VIKING SWORD AND SHIELD FIGHTING

A Step-by-Step Book for learning to fight with Viking Sword and Centre Gripped Round Shield. Incorporating safety concepts from an internationally known combat system practised world wide.

BEGINNERS GUIDE – LEVEL 3

By Colin Richards

VIKING SWORD AND SHIELD FIGHTING
BEGINNERS GUIDE – LEVEL 3

Published in Germany
Arts of Mars Books
Colin Richards
31020 Salzhemmendorf
Tel. +49(0)5153/ 80 32 53
http:// www.ArtsofMarsBooks.com

Copyright 2013 Arts of Mars Books

Author: Colin Richards
Design, Photos: Sandra Richards
Copy Editors: Krista Steichen and Charles Barnitz

ISBN 978-3-9811627-5-2
Printed in United Kingdom of Great Britain

All rights reserved. Except for use in a review by a reviewer who wishes to quote brief passages in connection with a review written for inclusion in a magazine, newspaper, broadcast or upon the World Wide Web, no part of this publication may be reproduced or transmitted in any form, without permission from the publisher in writing.

Neither the author nor the publisher assumes any liability for the use or misuse of information contained in this book. All martial arts, including historical can be dangerous and should only be practised under the guidance of a qualified instructor, for personal development and historical study.

ACKNOWLEDGEMENTS

In addition to the acknowledgements in the first book we would also like to mention the following people.

Again we must thank wholeheartedly both Melvin Raabe and Felix Seidel who put up with many hours of waiting and shifting position until a photo could be taken, as Colin was undecided which was the better angle! We took many more pictures than went into the final book. Without them this book could not have been finished. They are always enthusiastic and full of good ideas. Melvin and Felix are long-time students of the Arts of Mars Academy, and as such have contributed much to its growth and vitality.

As usual, my wonderful wife Sandra Richards who has without a doubt been the greatest help in keeping me on the course of finishing this book. Beyond that Sandra also accomplished the exacting feat of making the whole design and layout and taking all the pictures!

Colin Richards, Melvin Raabe, Felix Seidel and Sandra Richards hope everyone will find this book useful, and we welcome comments and questions.

All errors found in this volume are mine and mine alone!

Colin Richards

Salzhemmendorf, Germany
December 2013

CONTENTS

INTRODUCTION
About this Book — 6
Approaches to Combat Simulation — 6
Before you start — 6

SECTION I – GENERAL
I. 1. Historical Background — 8
I. 2. Important Notes — 9

SECTION II – MOVEMENT
II. 1. Alternate Weight Positions — 10
II. 2. Stepping to the Side — 12
II. 3. Backward Movement — 16

SECTION III – THE THRUST
III. 1. Thrusting with the Sword — 18
III. 2. Safety — 24
III. 3. What not to do against a thrust — 30
III. 4. Examples of thrusting — 32

SECTION IV – BINDING SWORDS
IV. 1. Swords in the Bind — 40
IV. 2. Applying the Concepts — 42

SECTION V – GUARDS
V. 1. New Guard Positions — 46
  Middle Guard and Plough

SECTION VI – OTHER ASPECTS OF COMBAT
VI. 1. Alternative Defences Against Attack to the Legs — 52
VI. 2. Fighting an Opposite Hander — 58

SECTION VII – THRUST DEFENCES
VII. 1. Defence against the Thrust — 60
VII. 2. Parrying the Thrust with Shield — 60
VII. 3. Parrying the Thrust with Sword — 64

SECTION VIII – SINGLE PERSON DRILLS

VIII. 1. Thrusting Against the Pell with Half Steps	76
VIII. 2. Thrusting Against the Pell with Full Steps	86
VIII. 3. Combined Cutting and Thrusting	96

SECTION IX – PARTNER DRILLS

IX . 1. Thrusting and Defending with Shield	104
IX . 2. Thrusting and Defending with Sword	108
IX . 3. Techniques Against Opposite Handers	114
IX . 4. Combining Parries and Combination Strikes	122

SECTION X – CONCLUSIONS

X. 1. Common Errors	146
X. 2. An Exchange of Blows – An Example of a Fight	150
X. 3. Conclusions	154
X. 4. Further Material	156

ABOUT THIS BOOK

This book contains the third and final volume of the Viking Sword and Shield Beginners Guides and follows on from the previous two books, both in mode of use and content. Here we add several new concepts and develop others that have been presented already. The main part of this book is the section on thrusting. We believe that people new to the art should have a full understanding of the basic principles, movements, and methods of control first before tackling the more demanding thrust technique. This is because thrusting, no matter what protection one is wearing, is inherently dangerous. Therefore we have tried to place special emphasis on the safety and control used in all thrusting attacks, and so this section is quite extensive. Some people may believe that we have been overly repetitive with our reiteration on thrusting safety, but this was our intention.

If you follow the section on thrusting faithfully we believe that you should learn easily how to thrust and how to do it so no injury occurs. A real sword with any sort of point at all will enter an unprotected body without much strength behind the thrust. Once the weapon is sharp, the effort required to penetrate the body will be negligible.

We suggest the student to remember these points when engaged in any sort of combat where thrusting is allowed.

We have planned a complete series covering all the main weapons of the Viking era. This series will be completed in an order determined by the feedback we receive from the people studying with our books and DVDs. So if you have a favourite weapon combination please drop us an email about your interest and we will consider that as a publication.

APPROACHES TO COMBAT SITUATION

This Book Series Supports Several Approaches to Combat Simulation. The principles found in this book can be applied to martial arts, stage fighting, fitness and re-enactment combat with only a little modification of the techniques, rules of engagement and the approach to targeting. For a more complete analyse of these different arts please see the earlier books. If the student is only interested in the technical aspects of Viking period combat and does not wish to fight, then the theoretical part combined with the drills will give sufficient information to pursue this aspect.

BEFORE YOU START

The Aim of the Book
Firstly, the aim of this book and all our books and DVDs is to develop interest in historical European fighting techniques. Though this series is called a beginner's guide, the techniques and concepts presented here will allow the student to fight without difficulty against people with more experience though with a poor understanding of the principles used in a fight. Usually people are self taught or taught false concepts and ideas by people that have developed their own tricks which work for them.

Secondarily we wish to emphasise the concept of control of the weapon, shield and the person. We have described in the first book, an excellent method of gaining that control and we suggest to all students to make control their prime concern.

How to Use this Book

This book is organised so that each section starts with a few notes that apply to every position in that section, often to the whole book. These notes are followed by pictures which follow in time sequence, from left to right. Most pictures have relevant text either above or underneath. The green stripe that is usually situated two thirds of the way down the page is called the Time Line, all pictures are situated on or near this line. This is so that the student can read the technique in the pictures as they would a normal sentence in a book.

Look at the pictures, read the relevant text and any other notes that are appropriate and then copy the movements as close as possible. Repeat as much as needed until the sequence can be copied. If notes are highlighted in red then these are summaries for that section.

Sign up for a newsletter at our website:
www.artsofmars.com

Grid Lines in the Pictures

Most pictures show a sequence of grid lines on the floor. These are there as a visual aid so that you can better see the distance and angles of steps. We have positioned the lines so that on the left side, when looking at the grid system from the side view, the distance from the first line to the second is a half step, the second to the third a full step. On the right hand side, however, this is reversed, full step followed by half. The third to the fourth is the weapon range to target. Note we do not always stick to these guide lines as our aim is visual clarity for the reader.

Help Videos

To give more help for those who find learning from a book difficult we have placed some videos on our Youtube channels which deal with Viking era sword and shields. We have set up a special channel for Viking era material. Our channels are called:
- Viking Guide Books
- Arts Of Mars HEMA

Watch out for our online learning program starting in 2014.

Organisation of the Book

As with each book in this series we have split the book into four parts: Introduction, Theory, Single Person Drills and Partner Drills.

Please note that students who wish to progress faster should modify the drills by starting in other positions, moving with larger or smaller steps and/or vary the angles.

Each part is broken down into sections, each dealing with a different aspect, so if the type of information changes so does the section. In the single person and partner drills areas, each drill is given a number sequentially so that you can note down the number and find that drill again.

Please note that this book is written in British English.

BEFORE YOU START

SECTION I – GENERAL
HISTORICAL BACKGROUND

Di Grassi

Di Grassi's treatise of 1594 in Italian and of 1597 in English, is one of the few works which feature a large shield gripped in the centre with one hand. See the previous books for his view point on how best to use it. In summary Di Grassi considers defending against cuts to be very easy and considers thrusts as the best method of defeating large shields. Most of this book is devoted to thrusting. We have again used information gleaned from the combat treatise of Di Grassi.

Di Grassi, generally, is wholly in favour of thrusts as a mode of attack though he seldom names the target of the thrusts. He generally has three Wards or guard positions, each of which can be used to attack from with thrusts. He basically sees the thrust as the most effective way to defeat shields.

This should come as no surprise as a sword being thrust presents only a small point which can easily pass by the edge of a shield, whereas the blade is a comparatively large area, so the shield is easier to interpose. Di Grassi's thrusts either go over the top edge, the left edge, or under the bottom edge of the shield depending upon which guard position he starts in.

We have also incorporated some techniques taken

from the oldest known combat treatise found in Europe, the celebrated 1.33 Tower Fechtbuch. This book describes a system of sword and buckler fighting which is very sophisticated though not overly complicated. From this treatise we have used several concepts and guard positions. For this book we have used the circular parry against the thrust.

We have also borrowed some of the technical terms and positions from the Liechtenaur tradition of German longsword.

IMPORTANT NOTES

You will also note that in some pictures the attacker or defender has no shield. This is to **facilitate the students view of what is taking place**, in the proper situation both people would be armed accordingly.

Other Weapons
We use the spear in the Common Mistakes section to illustrate one point. We will cover the use of spears in the future Advanced Guide.

Safety Equipment
We highly recommend the use of protective equipment whenever you take part in combat or training. This should protect delicate areas and especially the head, throat, spine, groin and hands. See the Beginners Guide Book 1 for further details.

Pell
The Pell is identical to that shown in the first book except we have added two more tapes in green. The uppermost indicates the arm pit or upper arm of the target. The lower level with the stomach or upper thigh. This is so that we can demonstrate that blows from above and below can be redirected to lower or higher targets. All tapes are positioned to the height of the person who is using the Pell relative to their body.

Recommendations
We recommend that you practice these drills with substitute weapons to save the blades of expensive steel weapons. Practice weapons are made from a variety of materials including wood, plastic, nylon, padded carbon fibre rod, and bamboo covered with leather. If you would like to see more information about these weapons please look at our website: www.Swordexperts.com

SECTION II – MOVEMENT
ALTERNATE WEIGHT POSITIONS

In the first book we advised that the weight should be kept equally over both legs as much as possible. However, there are reasons to vary the position of the weight while fighting. The first reason is that shifting weight is very much quicker than stepping. So shifting the weight onto the back leg from the front leg to avoid blows that are just in range to hit is a very quick and efficient tactic. By shifting weight to the back foot you can extend the distance from the opponent between 20 and 50cm/8 to 20 inch. Likewise one can quickly extend the attack range of any weapon by approximately the same distances, by moving the weight onto the front leg. These are the most obvious benefits, though there are others.

Do not move the weight too far forward or backward so that it is uncomfortable for your knees. These positions are also more difficult to recover your position from. A fighter can become stuck in positions where the weight is well forward over the knees. Trying to recover from these positions can cause serious injury to the knee.

Exercise 1

Weight in the middle. This is a very stable position.

While avoiding a blow by shifting the weight onto the back leg, the fighter as also prepared the conditions for moving the front leg backwards. This is useful if the attacker switches targets to the leg after his first attack missed.

Weight on the back foot. The weight is shifted so that about 60% is on the back leg. The position should be comfortable and not put too much strain on the knee.

Weight on the front foot. The weight is shifted so that about 60% is on the front leg. The front knee should be situated approximately over the shoe laces of the front foot. Further forward should be avoided.

STEPPING TO THE SIDE

Movement directly to the side is not common though sometimes important, especially if fighting in shield walls, or in skirmish lines where the fighter must maintain his lateral position in a fluid situation. We present two methods: a full step and half steps. Each have their advantages. Remember that width of step and the exact angle of the step can be changed due to circumstances or personal style.

The first stage in any stepping is to shift the weight onto the stationary leg and then move the other foot into position. With the feet about shoulder width apart and the body turned to the side slightly, you present a smaller target and extend your reach.

This step switches from the shield side forward to the sword side forward for the right handed fighter. The back leg could have moved to the right, further creating a greater angle to the opponent, which can be used to completely avoid their attack. Repeating the steps in the other direction would reverse the process.

Exercise 2

Full Step to the Side
Start in the normal stance. This step will be approximately 90 degrees to the side. This angle is not rigid and can be varied, though more than 20 degrees will be more diagonal in nature.

The back foot steps level with the front foot. This is the exact middle position. The weight should now be shifted to the right leg so that the left leg can move freely.

The foot that remained in place steps back to establish the normal stance. The original width of stance can be maintained or increased or decreased.

Half-Steps to the Side

Fighters sometimes need to keep the same side forward as they traverse to the side. This can be achieved by making a half step, that is, keeping the same foot to the front. Half steps are also called "gathered" or "fencing" steps. Remember that you can go right or left, make large or small steps, and start with either foot.

When going to the side you can move the front foot first or the back foot first. If you are making large steps and your back foot is pointing in the direction you want to go, this is probably the best foot to start with. If you are taking small or repeated fast steps, or you are going in the opposite direction of where your back foot is pointing, it is best to start with the front foot.

Generally, moving the front foot first is best. Repeating the steps in the opposite direction will create the other half of this exercise.

Exercise 3

Start in the normal stance, right leg forward. This step will be approximately 90 degrees to the side.

The front foot steps to the right. The width of step is dependent upon the technique or the situation. If the step is too wide, the fighter will do the splits, so take care, especially on slippery ground.

The rear foot steps the same distance to the right, returning to normal stance and maintaining the same orientation. To step to the left just reverse the process, the front leg going left.

BACKWARD MOVEMENT

The first volume covered half steps going forward, which has a multitude of uses. Fighters also often need to withdraw a short distance quickly while maintaining the same side forward. The backward half step is very good for this.

Tactically these are used to readjust your distance, retreat out of a difficult situation, or entice someone to pursue when it is advantageous to do so. Do not use continued backward steps without caution, and without knowing what is behind you. This can lead to disaster. When going backwards it is better to feel the ground with the foot as you step, if time allows. With practise this is easy to learn and turn shoes are better for this than modern hard sole shoes.

Do not forget to practice both left and right legs. It is advantageous to practice on a line so that you can see exactly how accurate you are.

Exercise 4

Start in the normal stance, left leg forward. For most this is the shield side forward. When using two weapons this side would be called the primary defence side.

Summary for Stepping

- When stepping a half step to side it is generally better to move the front foot first
- Side steps can be large or small
- At the end of a side step always orientate to the target
- Do not make a continuous step backwards
- Make small steps on slippy ground

The back foot steps directly backward. The fighter must feel with the stepping foot for obstacles and holes before the foot is grounded.

The front foot steps the same distance backward, returning to normal stance and maintaining the same orientation.

SECTION 3 – THE THRUST
THRUSTING WITH THE SWORD

Thrusting with a sword is an alternative to cutting with the sword, and is easy to learn though difficult to perfect. For a thrust to be effective it must be precise and accurate, striking the target at a good angle and with the correct structure in the arm, body and legs. If the stance is correct and the arm is aligned with the body, so the elbow is not sticking out, or that wrist bent excessively, the thrust will be accurate and strong. The real skill is to be able to repeat a thrust against a target and always hit the same target. In order to be accurate you need the correct grip.

Grip
Fortunately for Viking era swords this is the same as the grip we advised for cutting. The simplest of the thrusts to learn is the straight thrust, ending in an extended position, very often called the Long Point. Because the grip is always the same if the fighter can come back to the same position with the arm every time a thrust is made, he will build consistency in hitting the target.

A simple straight forward thrust against the Pell at stomach level ending in the Long Point position.

For thrusting we use the same resting point as for the cut. The main benefit for always having the same end point for the wrist is control. Keeping the wrist straight is also important because many Viking swords have small grips and the wrist can not be moved very comfortably.

This is the grip from the left handed person's hold.

Straight Thrust
This type of thrust is made by extending the arm out towards the target from the guard position, while aligning the point to the target. The eye watches the tip to the target. The stance should be stable and the sword point and sword arm aligned with the centre line. This is very difficult to show in these pictures but we will cover in greater detail in a later guide. After practice you can use peripheral vision to hit the target, and the process can be quite intuitive. Notice that the arm is not locked out stiff. This will be bad for your elbow and your opponent. This is thrust number 1.

As mentioned earlier, all fighting requires a relaxed posture throughout. Tension destroys the natural strength of the biomechanical structures created. Guard positions are structures that work for the user, and that is why the masters of old used particular positions.

The guard Long Point is the end position of the thrusts from Middle Guard and Plough. Thrusts from Ox can drop the hand into the Long Point position to obtain greater reach.

This is Thrust 1 usually from Middle Guard. From the Middle Guard position with the sword withdrawn.

The fighter steps forward with a normal step and extends the sword arm towards target. This position is usually called Long Point, or Langort in German.

Close up of the arm. The arm is not locked out. This is very important. This is a relaxed position, the biomechanical structure is good, it will not collapse without the fighter letting it happen.

SECTION III. 1.

Thrusting from Above

A more difficult place to thrust from is the Guard Ox, though with the correct technique it becomes much easier. Essentially in Ox, the sword arm is not in a commonly used position so for many it feels strange. Actually the sword is better aligned near the eye level, though the movement to extend the arm is hard to coordinate at first.

The grip is the same as before just inverted. The sword point should be aligned with the centre of the body. The swords reach can be extended by dropping the arm down into Long Point position or kept in the Ox position, depending upon the situation. The move from Ox into the Long Point position should take place at about two thirds of the way through the movement to the target.

This is Thrust position 2.
The fighter stands in the Ox guard with the sword withdrawn, the hand approximately just above the head.

After stepping forward with a normal step, the sword arm is extended toward opponent. This target is almost always in the upper part of the opponent's body.

Close up of the arm. The arm is not locked. This is very important. You can end in Long Point also by dropping the arm into position as you thrust. Again this structure is designed to be stable and requires a relaxed body.

SAFETY

Why is safety so important in learning combat? Most of the time the warrior is training to be good at combat, and therefore some of this time is spent training with a companion. Unless you have an endless supply of training partners, it is best to control everything you do so that they are not injured. Thrusting is the most dangerous of sword attacks in practice because it can lead to the sword entering the brain through the eye.

With this in mind, if thrusting is allowed then safety must be a prime concern. This means there must be sufficient protection, and the combatants must show adequate control, both in accuracy and strength. Compared with cuts, thrusts are relatively more dangerous to the person. We show some pictures of some key points below.

SECTION III. 2.

It is very important to keep the arm relaxed and not to lock the arms out on contact.

If sufficient protection is worn and the blade of the weapon is flexible, then the thrust can be quite strong. The blade shown in these pictures is far too stiff, even though it is sprung steel. Flexible blades bend easily and bow in the middle when put under sufficient stress. Care must still be taken because such blades can break during a thrust leading to sharp edges that can penetrate protective clothing. This is why losing control is not an option.

Keep your body weight in the middle of your stance and definitely do not put your weight in behind the thrust.

If the protection you are using is inadequate be ready to completely relax the arm and bend it with the pressure. Observe the example in these two pictures. The opponent stepping in onto a thrust leads to one of the most dangerous situations.

Control

The most important aspect of thrusting is the same for all weapon use and that is control. Control comes from practice and keeping the correct structure. Aiming and hitting the targeted area is essential, without which you cannot improve. When thrusting always pick a specific point to hit no matter if it is in a fight or just practice. When you have done enough you will notice that you no longer need to pick a target, you will automatically have chosen the point without thinking.

Suggested aiming points depend on the rules and the level of protection being worn. Full protection allows the face to be targeted instead of the more common stomach, left shoulder and right shoulder when lesser protection is worn. Once targeting these points becomes automatic, any point you choose will be easy to hit.

SECTION III. 2.

The highlighted areas indicate the target area used as an aiming point mentioned above. The face, the stomach, left and right shoulder. Try to avoid the throat and groin area at all times.

Natural Resting Position
We recommend using the natural resting position (NRP) as the best method to improve control and accuracy in thrusting. This is a consistent position that the fighter always comes to regardless of what move they have made previously. The most important thing to remember is to keep relaxed and do not lock up the arm.

Remember the NRP is a comfortable position, where the biomechanical integrity of the wrist is maintained.

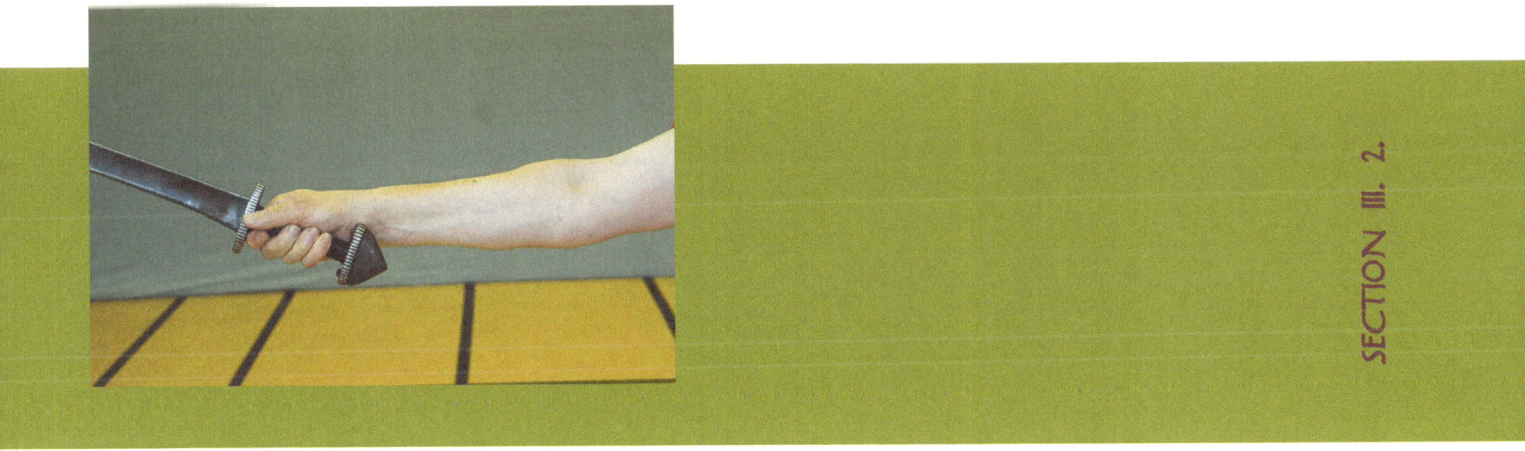

This is the NRP for right-handed thrusting in the Long Point position. The arm is still slightly bent and it is relaxed. The wrist should be straight at all times.

Target Vulnerability and Control
You can only improve your thrusting skill by constant practice. The ability to accurately hit any target you aim at is extremely important, though without control any thrust is dangerous regardless of protection. Thrusting to an unprotected area is inherently dangerous and should only be attempted if the area is fleshy and full control is applied. The first photo below indicates those areas that can be targeted if full control is applied.

Full Control
Full control is defined as a thrust that just touches the opponent's body, and then is immediately pulled off. A pulled blow has all the energy taken out at the moment of contact by pulling the hand holding the weapon back away from the target. If the opponent walks onto the thrust then the arm holding the thrusting weapon must bend with any force applied because of the opponent's action. Little or no energy should be transferred to the opponent's body. This takes time to learn but once learned it becomes automatic.

Vulnerable Areas
The second photo shows areas which should be avoided even if protection is worn. These targets are as follows: The head, face, throat, groin, inside of the thighs and the spine. These are delicate areas and can easily be damaged and protection failure can lead to serious injury. If you wish in your rule system to target these areas then make sure that full control is exercised.

Thrusting Short and Thrusting Off
These two techniques are used in different types of fighting. The first, thrusting short, is used in re-enactment fighting. This is when the thrust is made a little short, say one inch/2.5 cm, before reaching the full NRP, so that the weapon is stopped, then extend the arm to the NRP touching the opponent. This again requires practice but once learned it becomes automatic.

Unprotected targets that can be targeted using full control. Left and right chest, stomach, and front thigh muscle.

Thrusting off is used in stage combat and is taught so that there is no actual contact with the target, therefore it should be extremely safe. The thrust is simply targeted off line from the opponent's body, in a way that the audience cannot see there is no contact. Such an off line thrust can be extended into a full lunge so that it looks extremely spectacular.

Unfortunately there is one problem with this method. Because this form of attack is considered extremely safe there is a tendency to be either uncontrolled, or imprecise with the accuracy of such a thrust. From years of experience in many types of fighting, we have come to realise that full control and accurate targeting have to be exercised even while thrusting off to the side. Even though the target chosen is actually air, the attacker must be able to hit that target and be able to pull the blow if something should go wrong. The point chosen for such a thrust should be related to the body shape of the opponent, and that specific point should be set at a certain constant distance from the body part the attacker wishes to hit. We consider a distance off to the side should be about 12 inches or 30 cm. Good points to choose are: Level with the shoulder on either side, level with the stomach on either side, or the left and right breast muscle. The head should be avoided at all costs.

Protected targets that should be avoided, or full control exercised. The head, face, throat, groin, kidney area, inside of the thighs and the spine.

Points outside the body to use in stage combat as aiming points: Level with the shoulder on either side, level with the stomach on either side, or the left and right breast muscle.

EXAMPLES OF THRUSTING

Here are a few examples of good thrusting targets. They are places that the shield does not cover well, especially if the shield has be drawn out to defend another area by a previous attack.

Thrusting is usually the best method when targets appear for only a short time. The main difficulty being to orientate the hand in a way that brings the swordpoint on line with the target. It is good to mention that each guard position has its own best targets, and swapping guard position if your line to the target is blocked or difficult can bring new targets in line.

Thrusting from below can be particularly effective, especially against opponents with large shields. Quite often the large shield obscures the view of the defender against movements below the top edge. Di Grassi favours this type of thrust over all others and always steps with the thrust once or twice, sometimes with a full step followed by a half step, or some other simple combination. The direction of step he advises depends upon whether the thrusting sword is in between the shield and sword or outside of either. If on the inside of the sword and shield he tends to make a diagonal step to the left, if on the outside of the shield he tends to go to the right.

Thrusts to the right or left chest/shoulder, this is a common target, easy to hit. As shown, the left chest is excellent used against a left handed person, conversely the right chest is best against a right handed person.

Thrust to the stomach, low thrusts are useful to hit this target. This thrust can be even lower in the stomach area or the thrusting hand can be lower and the point of the weapon hitting at the same point as shown in the photo.

Thrust to the thigh, again low thrusts or thrusts from above in Long Point are useful to hit this target. Greater reach against the legs can be achieved by lowering the stance by bending the knees.

WHAT NOT TO DO AGAINST A THRUST

No matter what rules of engagement you are using or what protection you have, there are some actions that are not clever to make. Primarily these actions are safety oriented, though also they are not tactically sound.

First, never use a parry from below and thereby cause a thrust from a weapon to travel upwards within the frame of the body. This almost always leads to the parried weapon hitting the face, or throat. Always attempt to meet the thrusting weapon with the parrying weapon from above or from the side and deflect the point out and away from the body by the shortest route.

Second, never parry a weapon from one part of the body across a bigger area of the rest of the body, say from right to left.

For example, parrying a thrust against the right shoulder towards the left shoulder. This invariably ends up with the weapon hitting the centre of the body. Fighters do this because they only learn one parry technique, which is insufficient in our opinion

The thrust comes towards the chest, Red has the sword positioned below. Untrained people tend to simply raise a sword which is below upwards in an attempt to clear the thrust away from the target.

to deal with all the possible attacking lines of the thrust.

Third, always try to parry a weapon about 8 inch / 20 cm from the tip of the weapon, and not further down towards the hilt. This is particularly important against long weapons such as a spear or Dane axe. From experience, fighters, when first confronted by these weapons, tend to want to parry further down the shaft to ensure an effective parry. This is an incorrect assumption and we will deal with this problem in some detail shortly.

Summary for Thrusting

- Stay relaxed
- Do not lock the arm out
- Do not bend the wrist
- Aim at a target
- Never parry a thrust upwards in the frame of the body
- Never parry a thrust across the body from one side to the other
- Contact a thrust with a parry about 8 inch / 20 cm from the tip of the weapon
- Bend the arm if someone walks in on a thrust when not wearing sufficient protection

Some people, either in panic or without experience, parry the thrust up towards the face with the sword. This can, and usually does, hit the throat or face with unwanted consequences.

Similarly, some people parry so that the opponent's blade moves from say the left shoulder across to their right shoulder. This is very dangerous and tactically unsound. This is usually because the fighter has not trained correctly. The correct technique is to push the thrust off line in the shortest way that clears the frame of the body. Just because the blade is below on the left side, as in the example below, it does not have to sweep the attacking sword out to the right.

This would be the natural movement, though incorrect, if the thrust was meant for the defender's left shoulder. The thrust must be redirected out to the defender's left in this case. This is accomplished by raising the hand to the centre above the line of the attack and at the same time dropping the point of the sword The opponent's blade is swept from inside to outside, in this case from Red's right to his left, making a Roof Block position in Right Ox. The sword hand is moved from the right to the left just sufficient to deflect the thrust offline and no further.

It is important, as we stated in the first book that parries accomplish the defence with a least amount of movement as possible. The larger the movement the more the hand and parrying object will be drawn away from other targets which may be attacked in sequence by the opponent. Defending those other targets will become more difficult if the parrying hand wanders well out to the side or high above the head.

Red waits in position 5, Blue is in thrusting position 2.

When an attacker executes a tactical sequence designed to move the defence further away from the actual final target, parries that move in excess of what is needed plays into the opponent's hand. This is exactly how the medieval sword master Andres Lignitzer built his sword and buckler sequences. He finishes each set of techniques with one that the opponent cannot parry in time, because their defence has been drawn out of position too far by the preceding sequence.

This type of parry can also end up hitting the face, throat or the right shoulder region. This can all be avoided with the correct technique.

Blue thrusts for the chest on the left hand side. Red starts his parry from the left and attempts to clear the opponent's weapon to the right hand side. This is the longest route. Red is also slightly rising the point of Blue's sword by this action. This is incorrect technique.

Red has deflected the sword thrust into the face and must suffer the consequences of incorrect technique. Also clearly shown is the fact that the thrust is too late, the parry is more than half way down the blade, contact should be in the first 6 inches of the blade.

Reaching for an Early Parry
The following sequence shows how to make an incorrect parry of a thrust to the chest or face. As the thrust comes towards the chest, the correct technique with the sword point up is to circle the sword down on the weapon about 8 inch / 20 cm from the thrusting sword's tip. Here the fighter is attempting to do an early parry by contacting the opponent's weapon near the start of the attack.

Red waits in Guard Position 2, Blue is in thrusting position 2.

The thrust comes in but the parry is too late. By attempting to parry further down the blade, the thrust arrives before the parry takes effect. This is because the blade is extending forward as the defender is reaching for it. A very important principle is that something that travels further takes more time. This attempted parry lengthens the distance to the contact point, therefore lengthening the time before the parry takes effect, the thrust hitting home before it has been deflected.

The parry hits near the handle of the sword but the sword has already hit the throat! The parry should contact about 8 inches from the tip of the sword. All thrusts should be allowed to come quite near before being deflected so that the defender has the maximum time to form a proper defence. This also decreases the chance of the attacker's thrust being a feint.

Red makes a circular parry motion from above but reaches down Blue's blade to parry "early."

Red is hit in the throat. The consequences could be even worse next time.

Reaching for an Early Parry With Shield
This sequence is the same as the last one except using a shield to make the parry. Red is ready with the shield to make the parry. **Remember this sequence is showing incorrect technique.**

The larger the shield the smaller the movement has to be to deflect the on coming thrust. The problem here is not the size of the shield, but the intent of the user. Even a large shield used as shown in the pictures below would give the same result.

Standing with the shield so open may give the opponent a obvious invitation to attack. The defender on the other hand must close the line by the shortest route, when he is fairly sure what the target is.

Red waits in Guard Position 4, Blue is in thrusting position 2.

Instead of intercepting the sword at the tip, he wishes to be "quicker" and take the weapon further down the blade.

This fails because the sword hits the target before the parry takes effect. Note, if you parry just behind the sword tip you can leave the parry very late, because the opponent will find it hard to change line so late in the move, and they will be more convinced that the attack will strike the target.

Blue thrusts for red's chest, Red attempts to parry with the shield edge too far down the blade. This also leads to a very open shield position, which could also be exploited in other ways.

Red is hit in the throat and could have been hit in the face. He has failed to close the line of the attack with the shield edge.

SECTION 4 — BINDING SWORDS
SWORDS IN THE BIND

When fighting, it is important to know about the concepts of pressure and feeling. This is a vast subject though at the least a fighter should know the basics early on in their training.

Pressure should be present when two weapons make contact. If there is no pressure from one of the parties then their weapon can be forced aside and the opponent's weapon can push through. In fact, if there is no pressure after the initial contact, that attack has stopped entirely. So there should always be a slight pressure, and that pressure can be felt, hence the concept of "feeling." Feeling the pressure gives information. This information from touch is the quickest that the human body receives. It is this information that the fighter can use to his advantage.

In the simplest form, the fighter feels if the pressure is too weak or too strong. If too weak the weapon should be pushed or deflected out of the way. If too strong, the pushing weapon should be redirected, either by turning the hand slightly or by allowing the pressure to collapse the parry. This is accomplished in the second case usually by forming the Roof Parry positions so the blade slides away harmlessly to the left or right side. In its basic form, there are usually three types of sword binds: point up, point down and mixed. We show these in the following pictures. Generally the concept is the same in each situation, but the pressure of one or the other fighter is too strong, too weak or they both have the same

A bind of swords with points up. This is a very common position, and happens after parrying, or an attack that is parried or when using a counter cut.

pressure. We examine the weak and strong cases in the following pages.

The ideal situation for fighters with equal skill is that both use just enough pressure so that one can feel what the opponent is doing without the other able to exploit that pressure. Equal pressure should leave both fighters with equal information, and equal chances of countering the other's tactics in an ideal world. It is important to point out that, as noted in Book 1, swords and shields have weak and strong areas, in the sense of leverage. For a sword, the area from tip to middle is called the Weak, and the middle to the grip is called the Strong.

- **A fighter can still apply strong pressure with the Weak of the blade!**
- **Also he can be given weak pressure with the Strong of the blade.**

This is not a contradiction because pressure and leverage are not the same. If this is confusing it is possible to use the terms Soft and Hard for pressure, though we chose not to do so.

A bind of swords with points down. This usually occurs after parrying a cut from below, though there are other possibilities.

A bind with swords one point up and one point down. This is also quite a common situation, and occurs after a parry in Ox or by parrying a cut from below aimed at the shoulder or head.

APPLYING THE CONCEPTS

Weak

If the opponent's weapon is without pressure at the moment of contact, an attack or a vigorous parry will usually deflect it out of the way. Failing that, you can push through after the binding of the swords.

Pushing through the bind will usually illicit a sudden strong response from the opponent. If it does, then of course the correct response would be to go weak, take off from the bind and target another opening. There is another option which is to stay in the bind, change the angle of the blade, and thrust on an open line. This is known as winding and will be covered in the advanced guides. Generally, a sword weak at the bind will be deflected out of the way on contact. Taking advantage of this opportunity can be complicated, so we only cover continuing on to an open target in this guide.

If an opponent is giving a lot of pressure at the bind, that is Strong. The correct response, as we have noted, is to redirect that strength away by yielding with the parrying object. This is countering strength with weakness, though the weakness is controlled.

From a static binding of the swords, both players are feeling the opponent's pressure in the blade.

Blue has no pressure therefore Red pushes through the bind and hits an opening. We have left out the shields for clarity. The shield would cover the opponent's sword as this move was being made.

During this redirection there is still pressure applied and information gained, because the opponent may change plans during the movement. This is important and should not be forgotten.

Dynamic: when a strike has been parried and the parry is weak, or the strike is weak and the parry is strong.

Blue's weapon is weak and will be slightly deflected out of the way or the sword will be pushed out of the way, then Red's attack or parry should be carried through onto a target.

Strong

If at the point of contact, the attacker has pressure that is strong, the defender can generally guide the opponent's weapon away by releasing their parry, as shown in the pictures below. This is generally easier with a sword in the Ox Roof Parry. Usually when the opponent feels his sword redirected to the side, he will try to recover it or continue an attack to another target. This is when exchanging weapons is very effective so that this option is more difficult for him.

If the opponent feels weak at the bind, the correct response is to apply pressure to redirect their weapon out of the way. This push must be subtle or the opponent will feel it and respond likewise, thus the whole exercise is circular in nature, each player seeking to obtain the advantage. This whole process can be helped by correct footwork. If the pressure is to the right hand side of the defender, for example, stepping to the left brings the fighter even further away from the opponent's weapon.

Static: From a static binding of the swords, Blue has a lot of pressure.

Red lets the pressure through by lifting the hand slightly and allowing the blade to collapse in the direction of force, causing the sword to slide away safely. Red reaches a position similar to the Roof Parry in Ox on the left.

The exchange of weapons is also another way of exploiting strong and weak pressure from the opponent. If they are strong, this indicates that the best exchange should take place on the outside. If weak, this normally suggests an exchange on the inside.

When using the shield to parry, strong pressure will automatically swivel the shield to one side or the other, leaving the opponent either on the outside or the inside of the position, depending where the pressure was applied. This will be addressed more thoroughly in the advanced guide section on shield use. Keep in mind, both of these operations can be made with the shield against the opponent's weapon. The concepts are the same, just difficult to show in photographs. In shield and sword contact, the shield can apply pressure to the sword and the swordsman can yield to the pressure and try and redirect the force away from him.

Dynamic: Blue makes a powerful attack, Red feels the pressure at the moment of contact and allows the attack to slide past by collapsing the blade in a controlled manner. Red reaches a position similar to the Roof Parry in Ox on the left hand side.

This leaves Red in an ideal position to counter attack while stepping off line for increased safety. The shield could have been placed in front of the sword arm at the moment of collapse to defend against other threats.

SECTION 5 – GUARDS
NEW GUARD POSITIONS

Middle Guard and the Similar Guard Plough
This guard could be considered as a starting position, a place from where you can achieve any other guard position quickly and easily. This position is excellent if you have lost your shield and need to take up a good defensive guard. It is very flexible and can be used against thrusts and cuts. It does not matter which leg is forward, though it works better as a threat with the right leg forward.

The sword can be more withdrawn than that shown in the first picture; the precise position is one of personal preference.

The point is usually directed to the opponent's face or chest as a direct threat. Though another alternative is to aim the point at the sword hand of the opponent. Beware though, that the hand is usually quicker than the eye, so caution must be exercised.

Because of the central nature of the sword, this guard is useful in defence against thrusts. The point is well forward and therefore intercepts the thrusting weapon at a good distance from the body. Normally we advise that thrusts should be left till late in their path before we deal with them. Middle Guard is an exception. We can contact the thrusting sword early, stay in the bind and feel what is happening for most of the thrust. Then we can decide later in the thrust's path where to redirect. This is of course all in a split second and therefore has to be automatic. The final deflection is an example of

Middle Guard Without Shield
The sword is held in the middle with the point aligned with the opponent's chest or face. Either leg can be forward.

winding, which we have briefly mentioned. From the wind the fighter can also counter thrust. Counter thrusts are thrusts that maintain contact with the opponent's weapon during the movement. This alone is a large subject which we have no space to enter into in this volume.

From the left handed person's perspective.

From this position you can easily reach any guard position. Try this exercise out by moving from here to each other guard position and then return again.

This is Middle Guard, this can be with either leg forward, though left forward gives a greater reach.

Middle Guard With Shield

A shield, depending upon size, interferes with the position of Middle Guard so that it is usually slightly to the side, though it is still more forward than the Plough positions. This is an excellent position to thrust from. The forward sword position means the blade is usually faster to the parry and the thrust and so it is an excellent counter attack position. Other positions can also be easily reached from this position, making it a very good waiting position.

Almost everything that applies to Middle Guard without the shield applies with the shield.

In the 1.33 treatise this position is called the 6th Ward and is intended as a thrusting position.

The sword point is just past the rim of the shield and slightly to the right, aligned with the opponent's chest or face.

This is a good position to thrust or make a sword parry from. Again, a good exercise is to move to each guard position and parry from here.

This is Middle Guard, from a left handed perspective. Either leg can be forward, though left forward gives a greater reach.

Another view of Middle Guard from a left handed perspective.

Plough Guard

The Plough Guard is a little more withdrawn and sits on the left or right of centre with the point facing the opponent's face or chest. The plough positions are more leg sensitive as they present an invitation to attack the opposite side to the sword, which works better if that side is forward.

If the opponent accepts the invitation, one idea is to swap to the opposite side and parry and then either counter thrust if the bind is maintained, or strike, depending on circumstances. It is also possible to exchange the weapon by using the hand (if lacking a shield) or make a disarm.

Plough is also a good waiting position and can swap to most of the other guards easily. It retains some of the properties of Middle Guard and has some special quirks of it's own. Cut usually take longer to perform though thrusts are take about the same time.

The main use of Plough is to close off attacking lines and to invite an attack on the opposite side.

Plough Without Shield

You can vary the position from the middle to the left as an invitation. This is left Plough or Thrust Position 5. When made with a shield, the shield is probably best left covering the sword hand.

Or you can vary it to the right as an invitation. This is right Plough or Thrust Position 4.

The name Plough comes from the well documented German longsword tradition, and because that weapon is primarily used in two hands, it can be placed on either side reasonably easily. When used with a single handed weapon such as the Viking sword or axe in combination with a shield, the position is much more natural on the right hand side for a right handed person. The left side feels a little awkward at first, and its use is more limited because the weapon interferes with the use of the shield. We show it without the shield, add a shield in the left hand to make Plough on the left and explore the possibilities of its use as a guard of invitation. The shield can be held high, covering the head, or level with the sword, or below it.

Plough With Shield
This is the right Plough position, the sword is more withdrawn than Middle Guard. Plough on the left usually has the left leg withdrawn.

Plough also provides a good position to thrust or make a sword parry from. It also hides the sword more from the opponent's view.

SECTION 6 – OTHER ASPECTS OF COMBAT
ALTERNATIVE DEFENCES TO ATTACKS TO THE LEG

Move Legs

If someone targets your leg, it is best to simply move the leg back and avoid the attack. This type of defence is standard in medieval combat manuals. There may be reasons why the fighter does not wish to move back, so there are alternatives which we give here. Moving the threatened leg back is simple and quick and can also be used in a shield wall as the movement can be quite small. As a defence it is very effective and does not occupy the sword or the shield. The opponent's sword arm and upper body is then very vulnerable to counter attack. The classic medieval counter attack is to the head, as this is usually nearer and open.

Some fighters in order to gain more reach to attack the legs will lower their stance by bending the knees. This means that they will have their normal reach because it has not been shortened by reaching down to a lower target. In this case it is better to step back a full step, and to counter against their weapon hand or to step in and counter after their attack is spent.

Exercise 5

Blue, the attacker, targets the forward leg and the opponent either has no shield or their shield is occupied by another attack.

  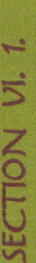

An attack to the legs is nullified by simply moving the targeted leg back, either level with the forward leg, this usually means you are in distance to counter attack immediately.

Or you can make a full step back. This will also lengthen the distance between the two fighters so that you might have to step to counter attack.

Using the Shield to Defend the Legs
This would normally be the preferred method if the fighter wished to remain in place, though we would always recommend that the leg be withdrawn slightly even if the shield is used in case of a follow-up attack. The second and third photos show a flat shield face. This is to facilitate catching the sword exactly on the central metal boss and is an advanced approach, especially if the shield has a large diameter such as 85 cm. The shield in the picture was used to allow the viewer to see more; though without advanced technique, this position is easier to counter. It is generally more useful to turn the face to approximately 45 degrees to the right, as shown in the Shield Parry section in first guide book.

The fighter intercepts the attack to obtain contact with the opponent's weapon. Using the information gained from feeling, he can decide what the next move should be. Knowing where the opponent's sword is, even if only for a moment, is an advantage for experienced warriors.

Exercise 6

The shield is at this moment protecting the left shoulder, the attacker targets the forward leg.

The shield is dropped a short distance to block the attack while the left foot is stepping back. This is double safe.

Not stepping back is an alternative usually used by people in a shield wall battlefield situation. Though even in battle line, a small step can be made. It is important not to get stuck into making only one response, but to experiment in training with other solutions to similar problems.

The last alternative is to parry with the shield while stepping in towards the opponent, and execute a counter strike to an open target. This requires good timing and likewise an excellent defence. This is of course the ideal solution to the problem and should take place in the middle tempo between the start of the opponents attack and the final end position.

Exercise 7

Or you can just use the shield and not step. In a combat situation the sword would have come forward here to strike a target, almost simultaneously with the parry. See the next picture.

You can also step in and counter while blocking with the shield.

Using the Sword to Defend the Legs
Sometimes it is tactically useful to parry with the sword, or you just have no other choice. Remember also that you could drop the shield down behind your sword to have it ready to make an exchange immediately as the parry was taking place.

Or you can bring the shield down on the outside and exchange there, though the leg must be withdrawn so that it is clear of the opponent's sword while exchanging. As a safety precaution, moving the leg is recommended whether or not the exchange is made. In circumstances where this is not possible ,the shield should be used to exchange immediately so as to prepare the sword for a counter attack.

The position at the moment of the parry is also exploitable by the attacker, Blue, who can also exchange by using the shield on the outside of Red's arm.

Exercise 8

The shield is at this moment protecting the left shoulder and head. Blue, the attacker, targets the forward leg. Red's sword is in Middle Guard.

> **Summary for Defending the Legs**
>
> - Moving the forward leg back level with the other leg leaves the opponent's head in easy reach
> - Moving the forward leg back a full step may take the fighter out of range to counter
> - Shield parries should use the face of the shield either with or without stepping
> - Sword parries can be used with exchanging for good effect
> - Sword parries can be countered by the opponent exchanging

The shield is left defending the shoulder, while the sword is turned point down and used to defend the leg using a standard Sword Parry 4.

The parry should be exchanged immediately so an attack with the sword can be made.

FIGHTING AN OPPOSITE HANDER

Fighters always unconsciously seek to defend the open side, and therefore they generally move to that side. When fighting an opposite hander a good tactic is to parry on the inside of the weapon. This positions your sword between their sword and shield. When on the inside of the sword, seek to thrust to the thigh, the arm, or the open shoulder. If the opponent parries with the shield, seek to hit the nearest leg by the shortest route.

SECTION VI. 2.

Both start in Guard Position 2. The right hander Red uses Attack 2 The attack is aimed at the left shoulder.

Green, the left hander, parries with an inside Parry 2.

Another idea is to bind swords on the outside and push the sword in the way of the shield and then exchange shield for sword, so that their sword interferes with the use of their shield. Exchanging weapons does not depend on speed, it depends upon timing. The shield exchange comes just after the sword contact, within a short period of time. This is called Middle Tempo.

If the binding is on the outside of the opponent's sword, then by turning the hand and adopting the Ox position, a thrust can be delivered towards the shoulder. If this is parried, the attack can be switched to the leg as in the example below.

Green steps forward and delivers a thrust to the right shoulder of Red, who parries with the edge of the shield using Parry 3.

Here Green, realising that the thrust is parried, cuts down to the thigh while covering the attack lines with his shield. Both legs could be targeted with this attack.

SECTION 7 – THRUST DEFENCES
DEFENCE AGAINST THE THRUST

There are specific techniques to learn when defending against thrust attacks. Fortunately they are easy to learn. With a duel weapon system such as the sword and shield, the fighter can defend with either the sword or the shield. Sometimes, that which the fighter uses is determined by the attack, at other times it is tactical decision by the defender.

In a battle line someone may thrust at the shield in order to occupy it, while a companion tries to penetrate the defence in another area. Generally though opponents will thrust at an open target. Depending on the target the fighter can decide which weapon to use. We start with the shield.

A thrust usually targets the right chest or the right side of the stomach because these are likely to be uncovered, either deliberately or by chance on a right handed fighter.

Another attacking alternative is for the fighter to cut for the uncovered area, in this case the left shoulder. If the opponent lifts the shield to block, the fighter cuts short and lets the point of the sword travel across the front of the shield leaving the point in

PARRYING THE THRUST WITH SHIELD

Both fighters are in Guard Position 2. Blue steps forward and thrusts.

line with the now open right chest and almost in the same motion thrusts to that target. This is one reason that shield movements should be kept small, so that quick changes of line can be dealt with.

The thrust targets Red's right chest near the shoulder. The initial movement of Blue's sword could have been a cut, which Red dealt with by stepping back a little.

Red steps back and makes Parry 3 with the rim of the shield, deflecting the thrust outside the frame of the body. Note that this movement is small, though we emphasized it for the clarity of the picture.

The shield is used with either the face or the rim to either block or deflect the thrust. Which ever is used it is important to maintain contact with the opponent's weapon as this gives very quick information about where the weapon is and what they are going to do next. If the attacker tries to circumvent the shield, this contact is vital, not only because of this information but the close proximity allows an immediate response to counter their movements.

If the left shoulder or chest is uncovered either deliberately or by chance on a right sided fighter, then a thrust might be delivered there. This is also quite common in a multiple threat environment, such as a shield wall or broken skirmish line.

In our example below, if Blue wished to continue this thrust attack, after the parry, he might change to Right Ox while stepping forward with the left leg and thrust to the now open right upper chest over the rim of the shield, or with a cut by dropping down and striking the leg. To counter this Red would simply drop his shield down or step back.

If Blue did change to Ox and thrust to the right shoulder, Red would then use the rim to deflect the thrust of line to his right. Blue could then follow the front edge of the shield and attempt to cut the forward leg of Red while stepping to his right.

Both fighters are in Guard Position 4. Red has lowered his shield exposing the left shoulder. Blue steps forward and thrusts.

The thrust targets the left chest near the shoulder.   Red steps back and makes Parry 2 with the face of the shield, stopping the thrust.

PARRYING THE THRUST WITH SWORD

A fighter can parry thrusts with the point down or the point up. Usually it depends upon the initial position of the sword which parry is best to make. The direction of the parry, either to the left or right is dependent upon the target of the thrust. So if the sword was initially at position 2 over the right shoulder, and the opponent's thrust was low on the right, aimed at, say, the stomach, then the parry would be point down sweeping from left to right. If the thrust was to the left shoulder and the sword was point up, the quickest would probably be a Parry 2 sweeping right to left. Learning all the combinations is a matter of training and experience.

The technique shown below is known as a Circular Parry and is especially effective because it parries on the outside leaving the defender in an excellent position to exchange shield for sword. It is important to note that this parry is not a strike, meaning it is not an attempt to smash the opponent's sword to the side. The parry must remain in contact with the opponent's sword so that it can be controlled. This advice is the same regardless of what weapon the opponent thrusts with. Whether sword, spear or two handed axe, the parry only requires contact so that the energy can be redirected away from the body. In fact, against a longer weapon the contact must be maintained until an exchange can be made.

Smashing down on a blade or spear only imparts energy to the weapon, which can be used by the

Sword Point Up: High Right Attack
Red the defender, is in the 2nd Guard Position, Blue the attacker is in Middle Guard.

attacker to help move the weapon to another line of attack. A better method is to place the sword on the opponent's weapon and then press the weapon down. This restricts their movement and makes their weapon heavier. In the battle line this action can tire out a fighter who constantly seeks to thrust on the same line.

The thrust is aimed at the right chest near the shoulder.

The defender circles the point of the sword down onto the thrust to sweep the thrust to the side. The parry contact should be about 8 inches behind the tip. It is very important to keep contact after the parry so that you can control the weapon and also exchange parries.

Sword Point Down: High Left Attack
This type of parry is most useful against a thrust aimed at the left side of the body as the defender has the most time to adjust his sword position. Also this sets up the shield to make an exchange with the sword, therefore freeing it to counter attack immediately. It does not matter if the attack was a thrust or a cut, the Roof Parry suffices to deal with both equally.

In the final position the exchange would take place normally on the inside. On careful examination Red has made a hip turn to facilitate this parry. This is indicated by the position of the foot; this is an advanced feature of the defence-counter attack transition.

Another interesting feature sequence shown following is that in the last picture, Blue could convert his Long Point position to a Right Ox and by stepping behind it, continue the thrust towards the face (if face protection was being worn), thereby continuing the threat and keeping the initiative. Red would be obliged to interpose the shield and also sweep his sword around his head, exchanging the shield for the sword and initiating a counter attack.

Both players are in Right Ox position.

Blue steps forward, the thrust is aimed at the left chest near the shoulder, Blue has converted the sword position to Long Point which has a greater reach than staying in Ox.

Red circles the point of the sword down before contact with the thrust and uses the edge to sweep the thrust to the left side. It is very important to keep contact after the parry so that you can exchange parries. Note the close proximity of the shield, which also covers the attacking line.

Sword Low: High Right Attack
The sword point is raised first, followed by moving the arm from the central position out to the right. Remembering to keep the point of the parrying sword as near to the centre line as possible, the hand moves the grip of the sword out just enough to deflect the thrust. There is no point in trying a circular parry from above as this may take too much time to execute.

This is an effective parry and leaves the defender on the outside, which again is the best position for an exchange of weapons. To better facilitate this, the defender in the following sequence could have made a half step back and raised his shield at the same time so that it was in position immediately after the parry.

Small positional nuances can make a huge difference in the effectiveness of a technique because of timing issues and distance; the smaller the distance the weapon must travel, the faster the action. Many people seem to underestimate the importance of timing and distance at the expense of trying to be fast, an error that needs to be re-learnt as one gains experience.

Red, the defender, is in the 4th Guard Position. Blue, the attacker, is in Middle Guard.

The thrust is aimed at the right chest near the shoulder.

The Red lifts the point of the sword through the centre line and parries the thrust to the right side. It is very important to keep contact after the parry to facilitate an exchange.

Sword Low: High Left Attack
This parry is basically a Roof Block in Right Ox formed from low on the right. The hand is raised with the point down and the sword swept to high on the left, deflecting the thrust off to the left hand side. There is no reason why the standard Parry 2 could not be made as well, except the hand would then interfere with the use of the shield slightly.

The parry leaves the defender on the inside so normally the exchange would take place there. A good preparation for the exchange would be to bring the shield up behind the sword so as to replace it immediately. For clarity we keep the shield back so that it does not mask the position of the sword in the picture. Blue on the other hand has brought the shield forward to protect the sword hand which is correct and does not interfere with the clarity of the picture.

Red the defender is in the Middle Guard position, as is Blue, the attacker.

SECTION VII. 3.

The thrust is aimed at the left shoulder of Red. The parry is again in the first 8 inch of the blade, and the deflection will be the least required to avoid being hit.

The Red drops the point of the sword so that the middle of the sword parries the thrust to the left side. It is very important to keep contact after the parry to facilitate an exchange.

Defending a Thrust to the Head

It is generally better to defend an attack to the head with the sword so that vision is not obstructed by the shield, though of course the shield is very good at the job.

The parry option depends on where the sword is, generally speaking. If the defender's sword point is pointing up, then it is easy to parry to the left side using Sword Parry 2.

If the sword is level, or pointing down, it is just as easy to raise the hand and, with the point of the sword down, sweep the thrust to the left side using the Roof Parry. This method is slightly slower so close in thrusts should be dealt with by using point up if possible.

Red is in the 2nd Guard Position, Blue is in Middle Guard.

The thrust is aimed at the head. Normally we would only thrust to the head if the defender was wearing a fencing mask, though in static pictures there is no danger.

Red makes a parry with the point of the sword up to sweep the thrust to the left side. It is very important to keep contact after the parry so that you can exchange parries soon after.

SECTION VII. 3.

Sword Point Level or Down: Head Attack
This is the Roof Block equivalent of the parry in Right Ox against a cut, though the timing must be correctly judged as the opponent's thrust must be gathered up during the sweep to the side. This is one instance where being too fast can have fatal consequences. The fighter must have the patience to wait for the attack to enter deep enough to be successfully parried. Also this parry allows an easier exchange of shield on the inside than in the previous example.

Thrusts that are only feints are going to change target if the opponent reacts too early. So the defender must wait long enough for the attack to develop to a point where an alteration of target is unlikely. This takes strong nerves and improves with experience, though it is better to practise this in training than to wait for the fight to find out the timing is all wrong.

Both Red and Blue are in Middle Guard.

The thrust is aimed at the head. Red prepares to step back and brings the sword high with the point down.

Red makes the parry stepping back with the hand high and the point down to sweep the thrust to the left side in the Roof Parry position. It is very important to keep contact after the parry so that you can exchange parries.

SECTION 8 – SINGLE PERSON DRILLS
THRUSTING AT A PELL USING HALF STEPS

This set of exercises is designed to develop both accuracy and control, while keeping the same side forward. This is a valuable skill to learn because of the advantages of thrusting after a parry or after a cut. Often in this situation the thrust does not have to travel very far to the target, compared to thrusting from a withdrawn guard position. Also you do not need to change sides, which is usually slower to do. Accurate thrusting reaps its own rewards in the end. We consider being able to hit a 2 inch 5 cm diameter circle every time a good standard, inside a 1 inch 2.5 cm circle is excellent. It is important to be able to do this even when tired, and regardless of the type of terrain or weather conditions.

Remember that the sword point should be aligned with the centre line.

Drill 1: High to Head. Thrust Position 1, Half Stepping from Middle Guard.
With a full body target, the head is an excellent point to thrust, though please remember that no protection is 100% proof against accident. Always attempt to hit exactly in the middle and with full control, so that the sword just makes contact, and leaves no impact mark. These drills should be repeated with either leg forward.

Drill 1

Red starts with the sword in the Middle Guard position and the left leg forward.

This type of thrust is easy to change to a different line if the opponent is about to parry the attack. Success depends upon timing and another target being available that is not too far away.

The defender should know which other targets are vulnerable and be ready to switch the defence to those places.

Red executes the thrust while making a half step in with the left leg.

Notice the arm is extended and the hips are turned in order to increase range and to align sword arm and right leg. The thrust is stopped on the target level with the head. Repeat with the right leg forward.

Drill 2: Thrust to the Chest or Shoulder. Thrust Position 2

This is a short range thrust, so you have to be quite near to the target. You can turn the hand down and use the Long Point position to increase range. This high line thrust is excellent to use to come over the rim of the shield, though this should not be attempted if the opponent does not have at least a fencing mask covering the face and head. In this position the arm is flexible enough to easily alter the point of the sword to find holes in the defence, compared with the position in Drill 3.

Drill 2

Red starts with the sword in right sided Ox Guard with the point of the sword orientated to the opponent.

By altering the point of the sword to the left or right, both shoulders can be targeted. These high line thrusts are excellent to combine with follow-up attacks to the legs, while stepping diagonally off to the sides.

Red makes a half step in with the left leg, while thrusting forward with the sword.

The thrust is stopped on the target level with the chest or shoulder tape. Repeat with the right leg forward.

SECTION VIII. 1.

Drill 3: Thrust to the Chest or Shoulder. Thrust Position 3.

This thrust is even shorter ranged than the Ox on the right and also awkward to do; you can turn the hand and make the Long Point position to increase range. This position is rarely used in sword and shield arts, though sometimes this is the only thrust you can do, especially if you have just parried with this ox. This thrust can also be used to avoid a Shield Parry as in the previous drill, though being more awkward, the desired result can be harder to achieve. The position is also biomechancally quite weak in the forward direction and hard to manipulate the point to over a shield rim due to the restricted movement of the elbow in this position.

Drill 3

Red starts in left sided Ox Guard with the point of the sword orientated to the opponent.

Using a half step forwards with the right leg, Red thrusts forward with the sword.

Red stops the thrust on the target level with his own chest or shoulder. This drill can be repeated with the left leg forward. This will be very awkward to do at first.

Drill 4: Thrust to the Stomach.
This thrust and likewise one from right Plough is very useful, and can sometimes come as a surprise as the opponent's shield masks it from view. Another useful target is the inside of the opponent's right arm if he attacks and leaves it exposed. If the opponent parries the thrust with the shield, sometimes a shift to Left Ox just before contact can circumvent the Shield Parry, though for this to work the fighter must close distance and therefore come deeper into the attack range of the defender. This will require good shield work to control the opponent's sword.

The thrust should start with the point of the sword being brought in line with the target, before any extension of the arm.

Drill 4

Red starts in Guard Position 4 with the sword under the right shoulder.

Red uses a half step with the left leg, bringing immediately the point of the sword in line with the target and then extending the hand, thrusting forward with the sword.

The thrust is stopped level with stomach target.

SECTION VIII. 1.

83

Drill 5: Thrust to the Thigh.
The end position is very similar to Long Point except the point is below the central position. Thigh targets become visible quite often in fight, and so learning this thrust can bring great rewards. This is another long thrust and as such can be used at maximum reach. Bending the knees during the thrust will slightly increase the reach as the target is lower than normal.

Remember the object of all pell work is to train the muscle memory, and to learn accuracy, among other things. The fighter will also learn to judge distance to a fine tolerance, and how to adjust stance and balance for different situations. The pell is the first proving ground for the techniques that will be employed in a fight. If a movement does not work well here it will not work in a fight.

SECTION VIII. 1.

Drill 5

Red starts in Guard Position 5 with the sword under the left shoulder.

Red uses a half step with the right leg, immediately bringing the point of the sword in line with the thigh and then extending the hand thrusting forward with the sword.

The thrust is stopped on the target level with the thigh. Repeat with the left leg forward.

THRUSTING AT A PELL USING FULL STEPS

Here we describe how to make a full step when thrusting at a target. This of course changes the side of the body that is forward and generally has a greater reach, though is slightly slower than a half step. This type of thrust is very useful as an initial attack, sometimes forcing a parry that opens up some other target, which you can cut to. See the section on combination strikes and try to make combinations which include thrusts in the mix.

Remember that we show all this work at the pell without a shield. Repeat all the drills while holding the shield and try to imagine where the shield must be to be able to deal with the most obvious counter attack of the opponent.

There are many ways you can start. You can start a combination with a thrust or a thrust after a cut. You can thrust after being parried or if you parry the opponent attack. We show some examples in this book, though this is a large subject in its own right.

Full stepping
From the Middle Guard, and Plough

Drill 6: Thrust to Head. Thrust Position 4.
The head is a fairly small target and people automatically move it if they think it is threatened. Quite often though a thrust from below on the centre line is not seen until very late. The major difficulty executing this thrust is having a clear line to the target as the shield is placed in the way most of the time. One possibility is to convert the thrust into an

Drill 6

Red starts with the sword in the Right Plough position with the left leg forward.

SECTION VIII. 2.

Ox position just before contact with the opponent's shield, though this will shorten the thrust, and the opponent must be wearing full face and head protection.

Also note that some people have trouble seeing a point moving towards them directly on the centre line. It is difficult to judge the distance in these circumstances and movements can be deceptive and hard to spot. Thrusting towards the eyes can exploit this advantage.

Red executes the thrust while making a full step in with the right leg.

The thrust is stopped on the target level with the head position. Repeat with the right leg forward.

Drill 7: Thrust to the Chest or Shoulder. Thrust Position 2.

Depending on which target is open, choose the one nearest the middle of the body, so that the parry must travel the furthest to be effective. It is possible to hit very small openings if you practice to improve accuracy. Never put all your force behind a thrust, not only for safety reasons but also targets can disappear quickly, so you must be able to swap targets rapidly.

By dropping the hand into the Middle Guard position as the thrust is made the fighter will end in Long Point which has a greater reach and is easier to change targets with.

Drill 7

Red starts in right sided Ox Guard with the point of the sword orientated to the opponent.

Red uses a full step with the right leg, while thrusting forward with the sword.

The thrust is stopped on the target level with the chest or shoulder tape. Repeat with the right leg forward.

SECTION VIII. 2.

Drill 8: Thrust to the Chest or Shoulder. Thrust Position 3

This is a thrust to the other side of the opponent from the last drill, though this movement is more awkward to do. It is probably better to convert this thrust into a normal Long Point position in the middle of the movement by turning the hand so the back of the hand faces right, thus increasing range and accuracy. Alternatively if the distance is correct the position of the Ox Thrust can be used to circumvent the shield. More on this in the advanced guides.

Drill 8

Red starts in left sided Ox Guard with the point of the sword orientated to the opponent.

Make a full step in with the left leg, while thrusting forward with the sword.

The thrust is stopped on the target level with the chest or shoulder tape. Repeat with the left leg forward.

Drill 9: Thrust to the Stomach
This is useful when the opponent has gone high to defend against, for example, a cut and you have time to drop the sword down below the shield face and thrust under while stepping diagonally to the open side. The opponent will probably lose sight of the sword during this process. This is very similar to the advise given by Di Grassi in 1594.

This target is often open in shield wall combat, though normally for the opponent on the right of the fighter's position, so the thrust must be made diagonally to the right. This also means that the fighter is open for attack on their right. This type of diagonal attack is known as Cross Striking in the re-enactment scene. It is very effective, especially with a spear.

Drill 9

Red starts in Guard Position 4 with the sword under the right shoulder.

Red uses a full step in with the right leg, immediately bringing the point of the sword in line with the target and then extending the sword arm, thrusting forward with the sword.

The thrust is stopped on the target level with the stomach. Repeat with the right leg forward.

Drill 10: Thrust to the Thigh
Quite often the thighs become exposed when shields are moved too much to defend against cuts or thrusts, so using a combination which ends in a low thrust can bring good results. Both thighs can be available as targets in the right circumstances, though the right thigh is usually a safer bet because the shield covers the left thigh (of right handers) extremely well. These low thrusts can be converted into high Ox thrusts during the thrust itself, essentially feinting one target and then exploiting an opening somewhere else. This will be covered in more detail in the next series.

Low thrusts can be difficult to see when using large shields. Sometimes the thrust to the thigh can be turned upward at the last moment so they contact the stomach instead, especially if the opponent stepped back with the target leg.

Again, lowering the stance by bending the knees extends the reach against the lower targets, though this also lowers the head of the thruster, causing it to become more vulnerable.

Drill 10

Red starts in Guard Position 5 with the sword under the left shoulder.

Immediately bringing the point of the sword in line with the target, Red then steps forward with the left leg and extending the sword arm thrusts forward with the sword level with the thigh.

Red stops the thrust in Long Point Position, touching the target level with the thigh.

COMBINING CUTTING AND THRUSTING

In these drills we combine a cut with a thrust. This is especially useful if the opponent steps slightly out of range of the initial cut expecting the attack to have finished. Also if the opponent's sword has been deflected, a follow-up thrust may find an opening. Even in contact with the opponent's sword, a thrust may still be used if the target is uncovered. Start about one and a half steps away from the target. Calibrate the distance by placing your sword on the target and then step back the required distance.

This is an example of keeping the sword moving, seeking to find another target, this keeps the initiative and puts the opponent in defence mode. All weapon attacks seek to continue the motion even if the opponent parries the action, or the target is missed. The threat of contact must be maintained.

Drill 11: Cut and thrust to the head

Drill 11

The Wrath Cut and Thrust: Head or Shoulder Variants

This name is taken from the German Longsword nomenclature and is a common technique in that context. If an opponent makes a parry with the sword that is weak, and the sword is slightly deflected, this can leave the attacker's sword point in line with an opening that can be thrust at. This sort of technique also requires a combination step. The cut is made with a full step and the thrust with a half step or sometimes with a full step. Therefore in each of these drills please calibrate at one and a half steps away from the Pell.

Red starts in Guard Position 1 or 2.

SECTION VIII. 3.

Red steps forward with the right leg and cuts to the head or right shoulder of the opponent. Imagine the opponent has slipped back slightly, the cut has travelled on so that the point of the sword is level with the opponent's right chest or along the centre line.

Red uses a half step with the forward right leg and thrusts to hit the chosen target.

SECTION VIII. 3.

Drill 12: Cut and Thrust to Right Shoulder
This cut is from the left shoulder and targets the opponent's right shoulder, as the opponent steps back and the cut ends level with the opponent's left chest. This is usually an excellent place to be against a left hander though not so advantageous against a right hander with a shield.

If the right handers shield prevents the thrust in Long Point the thrust can usually still be executed by changing to the Right Ox position, which should bring the point over the rim of the shield. This thrust is shorter and so will probably require another step to reach the target

Drill 12

Red starts in Guard Position 3 with the sword over the left shoulder.

SECTION VIII. 3.

Red steps forward with the left leg and strikes to the right shoulder of the opponent. As before the opponent has slipped back slightly, the cut has travelled on so that the point of the sword is level with the opponent's left chest.

Red uses a half step with the forward left leg and thrusts to hit the chosen target.

Cuts from Below and Thrusts in Ox

If, when cutting from below, you miss the target and there is no parry of the sword, it should end up in either of the Ox positions. Then using a half step the thrust can be extended to the target, and also you can turn the hand down and move into Long Point.

This situation could also arise from a parry of a cut to the head or shoulder, exchanged with the shield and then the thrust from the Ox position or into Long Point. This shows that there are always in combat, there are several routes to one particular position or another.

Drill 13: A Cut from Below and Thrust in Left Ox

This cut end facing the right shoulder of the oppnent, which is usually not protected by the shield. This is an ideal thrust to come over the rim of the shield, combined with a high line defence with the shield.

If the opponent had stepped back before the final thrust landed, the attack could be continued by either stepping forward a full step with the left leg or using a couple half steps with the forward leg.

Drill 13

Red starts in Guard Position 4 with the sword under the right shoulder.

Red steps forward with the right leg and cuts to the left thigh of the opponent. Imagine the opponent has slipped back slightly, the cut has travelled on so that the point of the sword is level with the opponent's right chest in the left Ox position.

Red finishes by making a half step with the forward right leg and thrusts to hit the target.

Drill 14: A Cut from Below and Thrust in Right Ox

This cut ends in Right Ox, so you are facing the protected left shoulder of the opponent; therefore you must choose a combination that has drawn the shield away from protecting the shoulder. This thrust can be quickly altered to target the head over the rim of the shield, if you are using a full body target rule set.

This position is good against a left hander. This thrust could also come from a parry of a cut to the head or right shoulder, after exchanging the shield on the outside.

Drill 14

Red starts in Guard Position 5 with the sword under the left shoulder.

Red steps forward with the left leg and strikes to the right thigh of the opponent. Imagine the opponent has slipped back slightly, the cut has travelled on so that the point of the sword is level with the opponent's left chest in the Right Ox position.

Red finishes with a half step of the left leg and thrusts to hit the target.

SECTION 9 – PARTNER DRILLS
THRUSTING AND DEFENDING WITH SHIELD

Drill 1: Using the Shield Rim
These drills are designed to improve a fighter's thrust attack and defence technique. The thrust should not be delivered if the target is not open, your partner must open up the target so that the thrust makes sense. This is essential for both players to learn from these drills. The attacker learns to target and be on line with it, and the defender learns the parry. You can vary the drills by making the target more or less exposed, or by starting nearer or further away from it. The shield has two surfaces: the face and the edge. Experiment with using first one and then the other to defend each of the attacks in the following drills.

Notice that this attack could have been initially a cut from Guard Position 2 that missed because Red stepped back a little. Or because Blue, seeing that Red had defended Blue's original target, shortened the reach of his cut so as to not contact the shield. So by ending the cut with the point aligned to new open target, say the right shoulder, he can continue the attack with a thrust.

To convert a cut into a thrust is fairly easy, though converting a thrust into a cut requires more movement and is therefore more obvious.

Drill 1

Both fighters are in Guard Position 2.

The defender in this case uses the shield rim to defend against the thrust. The movement required to make this parry is small, and large shields hardly seem to move at all. The key is to let the thrust pass the rim of the shield before deflection begins. The later the parry is left, the more likely the opponent will push for the target. This can draw them into a poor position. Of course the later the parry the more chance that it will hit. The timing of the parry must be learnt through practise.

Blue steps forward and thrusts for the right chest near the shoulder.

Red steps back and parries with shield edge using Parry 3, and pushes to the right, so the thrust is outside the body.

Drill 2: Using the Shield Face

This drill teaches how to use the face of the shield to stop and deflect thrusts. It is essential not to over parry and open up other targets. Remember that shields have strong and weak sectors, as shown in the first volume. The upper quarter in front of the face is a strong sector; this is the part that should be used to block. Low thrusts to the thigh should be defended using the lower strong quarter.

The defence shown in the last picture uses the face of the shield and the shield has moved slightly out to the left side from Red's perspective. This is a deflection element used to guide hard thrusts, especially from long weapons such as a spear, well past the shield.

Red stands in a very provocative position with both shield and sword low, leaving the whole of the upper body free to attack. Blue has a large number of targets to choose from, though they are all in the upper half of Red's torso. Red is pretty confident where the attack will fall, though not how. This is a risky approach and requires confidence and skill to pull off.

Drill 2

Both fighters are in Middle Guard position.

In the final picture of this sequence, Red could counter attack with a thrust to the exposed weapon arm, or thrust under the opponent's shield rim into the stomach.

Blue could continue by half stepping to the right and cutting under the shield to the leg. Or he could change to the Right Ox position while stepping forward and thrust over the shield rim into the face or the right shoulder.

Blue steps forward and thrusts for the centre of the chest. Red prepares his parry by raising the shield in front of him.

Red steps back and parries with shield face using Parry 2, and pushes the sword to the left, so the thrust ends outside the body frame.

THRUSTING AND DEFENDING WITH SWORD

Drill 3: Using the Sword Point Up
This section deals with parrying thrusts with the sword. You can parry with the point up as here or point down. We advise to step back at the same time though quite often in a fight this is difficult. Thrusts can often be avoided by even small movements, such as putting the weight on the back leg or using small half steps either backwards or to the side.

Generally these parries with the point up are identical as the parries against cuts as shown in the first volume. The same principles should be applied if possible, maintaining the point on the centre line and keeping contact with the opponents weapon.

It would not be advantageous to use this type of parry down by the stomach as the hand movement becomes awkward.

Drill 3

Blue is in Right Plough, and Red is in Guard Position 2.

If Red had prepared it beforehand, he could exchange the sword for the shield either on the inside, the simplest; or on the outside, more problematical, though possible.

Blue could step forward while changing to right Ox and continue the thrust towards the face, forcing Red to deflect even further to the left or to interpose the shield.

Repeat the drill with the thrusting hand protected by the shield.

Blue steps forward and thrusts for the left chest near the shoulder.

Red steps back and parries with the Sword Parry 3, deflecting the thrust to his left outside the frame of the body. Blue could protect his right hand with the rim of his shield.

Drill 4: Using the Sword Point Up

This is a good example of an invitation, positioning the sword where it can easily parry a thrust or cut. This has the added advantage of parrying on the outside, setting up a situation where the sword can be exchanged with the shield.

Exchanging is always a matter of timing, and has to be well prepared. Exchanging well depends upon training and experience, especially since many positions that look like an exchange is indicated, it is not possible to do so. This is one such situation, the defender has not prepared the technique because the shield is so far away from the sword that it will take too long to do.

Red can parry with the back edge of the sword or turn the hand and parry with the front edge of the sword. In this example Red uses the back edge.

Drill 4

Blue is in Middle Guard. Red stands in position 4.

We should note that we tend to exaggerate the parries so that they are easier to see. As the fighter becomes more experienced the deflections tend to be made smaller and smaller so that the defence becomes more and more efficient. This allows counter attacks to develop sooner and can leave inexperienced opponents wondering if an attack will hit or not, thereby encouraging them to continue a thrust to the bitter end.

Blue steps forward with a full step and thrusts for the right chest near the shoulder.

Red steps back and parries with the sword using Parry 3, pushing it to the outside of the body area.

Drill 5: Using the Sword Point Down

This is a standard parry technique which illustrates that the sword can deal with almost any thrust on its own as long as the technique is executed correctly. A safer and probably better solution to counter the thrust in the example below would have been to bring the shield down behind the sword parry to facilitate an exchange of weapons as soon as possible after the sword parry. This position is also parry 4 from the first book, which deals with both thrusts and cuts equally well.

An alternative defence to this comparatively low thrust would have been to come from above and have made a circular parry, sweeping the sword out to the right hand side allowing an exchange on the outside.

Drill 5

Both fighters are in right Plough Guard position.

The final picture shows that Red is just not moving the arm to facilitate the parry. He is turning the whole body, using the hips and shoulders combined with a small step backwards. The whole body is coordinated in the movement. Even though not much power is needed to deflect a thrust, this movement promotes good structure, and the coordination needed to deal with hard blows.

Blue steps forward and thrusts for the stomach. Red prepares to use the front edge of the sword to make the parry, putting the point down and sweeping the hand from right to left.

Red steps back and parries using the sword edge with the point down in Parry 4, and pushes the thrust to the left, so the thrust is outside the body frame.

SECTION IX. 2

TECHNIQUES AGAINST OPPOSITE HANDERS

Remember that both players can do these attacks on each other, just mirror the drill positions. Also in each of these positions the initial attack must be against an opening. This means your partner should open up the target deliberately so that you can practice in the correct manner.

Drill 6: Combination to the Right Thigh
Green attacks to provoke a response, he is prepared for any answer. In this case Blue uses the sword to parry which is perfectly reasonable to do. Had Blue defended this initial attack with the shield, Green could continue with the second attack as shown in this drill, or he could have changed to left Ox position and thrust in towards the face or right shoulder of Blue. Had Blue slipped backwards with a step, Green could have ended in Long Point and then stepped forward thrusting to another open target.

Drill 6

Both combatants are in Guard Position 1. They could be in any guard position. Try others.

Green attacks the head of the opponent, stepping forward.

Blue makes several mistakes in this situation, which can all be corrected. In a fight situation, Blue could parry the last attack with the shield, or he could have stepped back slightly. Alternatively he could have stepped behind his left leg with his right leg while parrying with the shield, turning to the right slightly.

The final picture shows Green covering the expected attack lines of Blue. Green could equally exchange shield for sword instead, depending upon the timing and position.

Blue parries with the sword in the Ox position. This exposes the whole left side of the fighter, though this is not in itself bad.

Now half stepping to the right, Green cuts to the leg from above, covering the opponent's attacking line with his shield.

Drill 7: Combination to the Right Shoulder
This is a good example of a cut being changed into a thrust to defeat the shield. Here it takes place in two stages, though it is possible to do this instantaneously on contact with the opponent's shield. This is one of the most useful aspects of the Ox position, and should not be underestimated.

Also note how low a parry with a shield can be to stop a blow to the head when using the rim. In some circumstances this can be a disadvantage, and care should be taken when doing this type of block.

Drill 7

Both combatants are in Middle Guard position. They could be in any guard position. Try others.

Green cuts to the head of the opponent, stepping forward.

How the sword is orientated to the shield is very important and can lead to some surprising results. This an interesting subject in its own right and we will examine the effects of change orientation in the advanced guides.

Because Blue still has contact with the sword of Green, he could parry the thrust with the shield rim. This would be a comparitively large movement of the shield compared to dealing with a cut, thus drawing the shield defence away from other targets. Green could use the sequence shown in the last drill to finish.

Blue could continue the drill and parry the thrust with the sword, and Green could then repeat the last attack from the previous drill to finish the position.

Blue parries with the shield. This leaves the sword to counter attack with using a low thrust, except...

While half stepping to the left Green thrusts to the shoulder while covering the opponent's attacking line with his shield rim.

Drill 8 Combination from Low to High
Because opposite handed people operate with their sword on the unshielded side of the opponent, there are many targets to choose from. This combination engages the opponent's sword low and exploits the large opening above. This is a theme we have touched on many times in these books, and this is an excellent example. You will notice that Blue failed to step back so he was in danger of being hit right from the start. Because of Blue's static nature, Green can manoeuvre to the side and exploit all the advantages that brings.

We cannot emphasise enough how important even small movements off the centre line relative to the opponent are. The more experience a fighter has the more small angles changes and distance adjustments alter the possibilities to advantage.

Drill 8

Both combatants are in Guard Position 4. They could be in any guard position. Try others.

Green attacks the right thigh of the opponent, stepping forward.

Remember, the shield should be seen as a weapon and the opponent's attacking possibilities with this usually passive object should also be noted. We will cover this topic in advanced guides. Notice that in the third picture Green as covered himself well with the shield preventing Blue from attacking with the shield should he have wanted to. In the last picture Green protects himself from a shield attack by using distance by stepping off to the side, and from the sword attack by again covering the line with the shield.

Blue parries with the sword using Parry 5.

While half stepping to the left, the fighter cuts to the right shoulder, while covering the opponent's attacking line with his shield.

Drill 9: Combination to the Stomach
Using Guard Position 5 is not easy against a similarly handed person, though against an opposite handed one it is even harder. Your timing must be good. Here Blue has failed to step back in response to the attack and since the opponent is left handed, the shield parry has obstructed the use of his own sword. This means all attacking lines are closed down by Green because of where he positions the shield at the end of the technique.

Drill 9

Both combatants are in Guard Position 5. They could be in any guard position. Try others.

Green attacks the right thigh of the opponent, stepping forward.

A fighter must always be aware of what starting position the opponent is in when initiating an attack. Some positions have definite disadvantages against others especially if the opponent gains the initiative as in the example shown here. Becoming knowledgeable about which position is best in which situation is often a matter of experience and analysis. Here is an excellent example of a poor result coming from an inadequate starting position. The problem is compounded by the opponent being opposite handed.

If Blue continued the drill by parrying the thrust with the shield under the sword arm, Green could then attack the right shoulder from below or above or even drop the sword to cut the thigh from above.

Blue parries with the face of the shield. This leaves the sword to counter attack, except the sword has been somewhat masked by the shield defence. This helps Greem maintain the initiative.

While half stepping to the left Green thrusts inside the shield to the stomach, while covering the opponent's attacking line with his shield.

COMBINING PARRIES AND COMBINATION STRIKES

Counter Attack Using Alternative Stepping to the Side.
We look at the further drills for using combination stepping, where the defender can utilise a side step to gain advantage for a counter attack. These situations are rare but at certain times variations in stepping angle and size of step can create advantages. These examples are presented to widen the experience and demonstrate that combining steps with different attacks can bring about situations where the opponent is technically beaten. The art is developing the timing to make the attack happen in the moment when the opponent has no viable defence.

Drill 10: Counter Attack to the Weapon Arm
A simple side step with devastating results. Blue can be criticised for lazy shield work. Though experience shows that this lazy shield use is quite common. Of course if he had moved the shield to defend the arm, then something else would have been exposed and Red is in the ideal position to exploit that. This is the magic of combat!

Drill 10

Both start in Guard Position 1.

Red moves in the middle tempo before Blue completes his cut and before his shield defends the open target, the sword arm. The subtlety of the side step is seen. This off line movement has probably made it impossible for Blue to reach Reds leg under his shield, thereby negating his most natural continuation of the attack, even if he had parried the arm attack with his shield.

If Reds arm attack had been parried with Blue's shield, he could have moved diagonally to the right and attacked Blue's leg.

Blue attacks Red in the head, stepping forward with a full step. Red starts to step to the right side.

Red steps to the right side parries with the shield using Parry 1, at the same time cutting to the right arm of the opponent.

Drill 11: Counter Attack to the Right Leg
Blue seems to have learnt one lesson in this drill. As noted in the last drill he now has defended the exposed arm with the shield as he attacked. Red simply switches targets to the thigh. This illustrates one of the key principles of combat, a flexible relaxed response to every situation, leads to opportunities. To become relaxed in a fight depends upon how much repetition and practice has been done and on the disposition of the person. An absolute desire to win at any cost is counter productive to this flexibility.

Do not become fixed on one object, such as winning, be flexible, especially in the face of determined defence. Some people make many mistakes attacking a good defender, some break under pressure.

Drill 11

Both start in Guard Position 2.

Red executes the same movement as in the last drill in the third picture, though this time because Blue has at last learnt to defend the sword arm, Red attacks the leg instead.

Red covers the high lines of attack with his shield because these are the routes to the nearest targets. This almost forces Blue to seek targets below the shield, which because of geometry, are further away. With Red stepping off the centre line, these lower targets are almost certainly out of distance.

Blue attacks Red in the left shoulder, stepping forward with a full step. Red starts to step to the right side.

Red steps to the right side, parries with the shield using Parry 2, at the same time cutting to the right leg of the opponent from above or below.

Drill 12: Thrust Counter to Chest, Between the Shields

We have swapped to the larger shields to demonstrate that even with large shields which obstruct a lot of targets and hinder movement, targets can be found. In the example, Blue's right arm was also exposed and could have been attacked. Shield size is usually a personal preference, the larger shields need to be practiced with to see how they are best used.

When using the larger shield, Guard Position 3 is probably not the best starting position to use. The book is structured so that it covers most of the positions that have been recommended, and as this example shows, many alternatives are possible even in unfavourable circumstances. Generally the recommendation is to use positions that are easier to develop attack from. With a large shield all guard positions on the left hand side are more difficult to use.

Drill 12

Both start in Guard Position 3.

If Blue would have used the shield edge to parry the thrust, Red could have stepped to the right with a diagonal step and cut for the thigh, flowing under the shield's right hand side to the bottom edge. If Blue avoided this, Red could have stepped forward and thrust under the shield edge into the stomach, in the manner of Italian master Di Grassi.

Blue attacks Red in the right shoulder, stepping forward with a full step. Red starts to step to the side.

Red steps to the left side and a little forward while blocking with his shield edge, then thrusts Blue in the chest between the shields.

Drill 13: Cut to the Thigh from Above.
Again a repeated theme. Once you have seen some techniques, the patterns will become familiar. How the patterns combine will also become obvious as you practice. This will eventually lead to instantly recognising a pattern and knowing how to change it to your advantage. The more experience you have, the easier it will become.

Again one can criticise Blue for not dropping the shield, or he could have stepped back again, though as the shield covers one area, other areas are opened up. The dilemma is to predict what the opponent's next move will be and to be one step ahead in the guessing game. There are always reasons why people do certain movements and defences and it is part of the art of combat to force the opponent into making bad decisions and mistakes.

Had Blue dropped the shield down quick enough, Red would again switch to an open target, such as the sword arm or left shoulder, or he could drop his stance right down and attempt to turn the sword under the bottom edge of the shield. He could advance further to the right and try and get behind the shield, or if Blue turns, maybe he has time to change to the other side entirely. All these variants should be automatic without having to think them through.

Drill 13

Both start in Guard Position 4.

Blue chooses the low line to attack on this time, and Red counters by covering this line with his shield and attacking the thigh himself. Blue has failed to use his shield, which is obviously an area he needs to work hard on! Had he defended the attack with the shield, Red could continue the attack on the high line while moving diagonally to the right.

Blue attacks Red in the left leg, stepping forward with a full step. Red starts his sidestep to the right.

Red steps to the right side, parries with the shield using Parry 4, at the same time cutting to the right thigh of the opponent from above.

Drill 14: Cut from Above Against the Sword Arm

Generally speaking sidesteps bring you out of range of the opponent while you remain in. This is only if the sidesteps are small because they rapidly move away from the opponent if they are wide. We show an example of this happening in our Common Mistakes page later in the book.

Look for opportunities to step to the side like this one, they are quite common positions. Even if Blue could have blocked this attack with the shield, Red can add further pressure by moving to the left using half steps. Should Blue also turn, Red can again switch, moving to the right again, placing his shield on the opponent's shield and masking his sword. We have mentioned and shown so many examples that the method, concept and execution should be familiar by now.

The side step shown in this example is very subtle and yet it changes the situation dramatically. Footwork is the basis of all tactics and the engine that drives all techniques. Footwork allows the correct positioning of the body to the opponent according to the situation. It is this positioning that exploits the advantages of geometry in the movers favour, advantages that are tangible and measurable. It is timing that ensures this geometrical advantage takes place before the opponent can react and alter the situation to neutralise it.

Drill 14

Blue is in position 5 and Red is in position 3.

Red could have chosen several targets in the final picture, such as the head or the sword hand. He could have also struck with the point up depending upon the size of his shield. Notice that Red has also oriented his centre line on the target by turning lightly to the right from straight ahead to maximise power.

Blue attacks Red in the right leg, stepping forward with a full step. Red begins his sidestep to the left.

Red steps to the left side while blocking with his shield using Parry 5 and cuts down on the right shoulder or arm of Blue from the outside.

Drill 15: Countering the High Line Parry

Very often making a parry leads to a position where a good counter attack is possible. There may also be a chance to exchange the parrying weapon and therefore switch sides from inside to outside. The number of possibilities are seemingly endless. We present a few examples from which you can develop your own derivatives to suit your fighting style.

The student should remember that to make any technique successful, timing is essential; speed is of secondary importance. Also there are efficient ways of executing moves and inefficient ways, usually the shortest route is best. The fighter should always look for the shortest way to achieve the effect they desire and eventually through experience this will be easier to do. The sequences we show are short, sometimes because they are short sequences in their own right and sometimes for space and clarity. Short sequences are easier to learn and by combining several sequences from the book the reader can create complex situations merely by adding a block or two, followed by a counter attack.

Drill 15

Both combatants are in Guard Position 1. Blue attacks the head while stepping forward.

Red uses Parry 1 with his shield, counter attacks against Blue's right shoulder while making a half step forward.

In this drill Red sets up Blue with his first attack, drawing the shield away from protecting his lower left side. With his second attack, he goes for the lower opening, the left thigh while stepping offline away from Blue's sword side.

See the fight at the end of the book for a long sequence.

Blue defends the attack with the shield using Parry 2 while half stepping back.

Red then makes a diagonal step to the right using attack 4 to Blue's left thigh.

Drill 16: High Line Counter Thrust with Low Line Finish

We include an exchange of shield for sword in this drill. The exchange controls the opponent's sword at the crucial moment when we wish to free up the sword to counter attack. Without this swap and control you could be open to another attack after your sword loses contact. In the dynamic world of combat, moments of control are short lived and rare, so when they occur you have to take maximum advantage of that situation.

In this example the moment of control at the exchange point is converted into a thrust over the shield to the chest, forcing Blue to defend with the shield. At this point both Blue's shield and sword are occupied, leaving Red to safely move to the outside and attack another target, in this case the thigh. It is not important at this stage if this attack is successful, the real point is that this attack is made for free with little danger to oneself. Even if Blue extracts himself from this situation, this free attack is a real psychological pressure that can be built into a winning advantage. Behind all correct technique application there is a psychological element that cannot be ignored.

Drill 16

Both combatants are in Guard Position 2. Red invites an attack to the left shoulder.

Blue attacks the left shoulder while stepping forward. Red parries using the sword with a Roof Parry,

Red exchanges shields on the inside and counter thrusts with the sword in Ox against Blue's right shoulder while stepping in with a half step forward.

Remember that highly skilled opponents will be constantly seeking opportunities to counter attack even under immense pressure. So the most important aspect of all these combinations for a fighter is to maximise their own defence at every moment in the fight while maintaining possibilities of finishing the fight. Manoeuvre is the easiest way to ensure this, coupled with sure defence. The attacker can be neutralised by good positioning and closed out by skilled defensive moves. This can be very frustrating, having every attack stifled before it is complete.

Drill 16 continued

Blue defends the attack to the shoulder with the shield using Parry 2 while half stepping back.

Red then makes a full step diagonally to the right using Attack 4 to the Blue's left thigh.

Drill 17: Switching from the High Line to the Low

Footwork is so important in combat that we advise our students to repeat the basic steps and combinations of step regularly. Good footwork allows the fighter to avoid blows and thrusts without the benefit of a parry, change sides in an instant and to manoeuvre round the opponent at will. Unfortunately the other fighter is trying to do the same, so that it can all become confused, that is why we practice.

We try to isolate certain movements in these drills so that they can be followed and the principles learnt by repetition. We try not to make them too complicated, so that the principles are obvious. You can add complexity as you wish. To extend a drill just change the result at the end point by replacing the hit with a defence and add more attacks and counter moves. Keep these movements simple or the thread of the drill will be lost!

Drill 17

Both combatants start in Guard Position 3. Blue makes a step and attacks Red's right shoulder.

Red has parried with the sword in the picture below in order to exchange shield for sword if the circumstances are right. The parry has left Blue's sword quite high so that there is plenty of space under the blade to slip the shield into. This means, had Red wished he could have exchanged shield for sword either on the inside or the outside. The outside is usually better in one on one fights, though in multiple opponent situations Red may have preferred to exchange on the inside and stepped to his right, thus avoiding the attack of other combatants. Sometimes we are forced by circumstance to modify tactical choices even if this leads to a sub-optimal result.

This is a simple example of fighters being channelled into various manoeuvres because of terrain, other team members or the actions of multiple opponents. It is common in a multi-threat environment and is mainly learnt through experience. These outside influences are to be expected, though dealing with these extra concerns, over and above the simple exchange of blows can overload the fighter, leading to defeat.

The aim of training and practise is to make movement, technique and tactical decision making auto-

Drill 17 continued

Red parries with sword Parry 3, while remaining in place.

Red exchanges the sword with the shield on the outside...

matic. The fighter can then deal with the unexpected as it comes along because his head is not filled with other considerations. Through experience the number of unexpected happenings will reduce and everything will become much easier.

If the fighter is also in command of other fighters it is essential that all other aspects of the fight are automatic, so that he has time to command the group. Command is a difficult task, especially in small skirmish groups where the commander must fight at the same time as overseeing the progress of the battle.

This drill illustrates an interesting manoeuvre where Red steps to the right while cutting under both the sword and the shield of the opponent. This is a switch of side and of high to low line, the attack can be countered quite easily with the sword or shield, though by transferring to the right side Red keeps the initiative and pressure. Red's shield is in the perfect position to nullify most of Blue's short term counter attack options.

...and steps forward, attacking Blue's right shoulder. Blue steps back and parries with Sword Parry 3.

Red makes a diagonal step to the right and cuts under Blue's sword to whichever thigh is easiest to hit using Attack 5, covering Blue's attacking lines with the shield.

Drill 18: Thrusting on the High Line, Cutting to the Low

Nearly all fights which do not end immediately, flow backwards and forwards, with one combatant having the initiative then the other. This is a natural state of affairs, though not something a fighter wants. With people of similar skill our main problem in combat is to convert the initiative into a winning move. This can be difficult; the trick is to have patience, and not to rush to win. To advise patience in a full speed encounter sounds strange, but behind this advise is the fact that this is the best method to convert an advantage into a win. Rushing to hit an opening that the opponent knows is open and who is pretty sure you are going there next is bad tactics. Better is to strike quickly but with enough time to change to another opening that has appeared because the opponent needs to close the obvious one. This will all become apparent with more experience.

Drill 18

Both combatants are in Guard Position 4. Blue attacks Red's left thigh making a full step.

One of the best ways to improve is to prepare set piece combinations that flow seamlessly from one attack to another. First try learning combinations of three, then four and finally five cuts or thrusts in a row, all the time being able to defend yourself with the shield. These continuous combinations grow in momentum and lead to excellent chances of winning the fight. They must flow automatically and be changeable during the combination, maybe to enter another sequence or to pause for defence, before taking up the combination again.

For example, starting with a cut to the right shoulder and dropping down to cut the right leg, then cutting through to Right Ox and thrusting into the left shoulder, followed by stepping diagonally to the right and cutting from above onto the left leg. This four-move combination could then be followed by another three-move combination and so on. This is when all the drill practise with different cuts and thrusts starts to pay off.

Red takes a half step back, parries with the shield using Parry 4.

Red thrusts with the sword, using Thrust 2, attacking Blue's right shoulder with a half step forward. Blue makes a step back and parries with the Shield Parry 2

Another consideration to remember is that with these developed and practised combinations, it is timing not speed that is important. In reality, a sharp sword does not have to be "stunningly" fast to do considerable damage, the fighter must only be well coordinated and accurate. Just as powerful muscles and hard hits are not as important as the coordination of the whole body behind the strike.

Drill 18 continued

Red makes a full step diagonally forward to the right, covering the attacking lines with his shield.

Red uses Attack 4 against the left thigh, while simultaneously blocking Blue's Thrust 2 in Right Ox.

Drill 19: Thrusting on the High Line, Cutting to the Low

Pushing yourself hard to win a fight quickly is the wrong approach, even if you have little time before someone else joins the opponent leaving you out numbered. Generally it is better to go no faster than normal and continue your normal tactics, exploiting the initiative and striking for openings.

Drill 19

Both combatants are in Guard Position 5. Blue makes a full step and attacks Red's left thigh.

Red steps a half step back, parries with the sword.

A Note About Fighting Multiple Opponents

Fighting more than one opponent is actually no more difficult from a combat point of view than fighting one. The main problem is correct positioning so that both opponents are unable to attack you at one time. So you should always manoeuvre so that you are fighting one opponent at a time. The movement to do this is quite subtle, and relies on the knowledge that two people apparently operating together do not usually do so. You can distract one with a feint attack, who will usually step back or stop and then carry that attack on to hit or stop the second person while stepping away from the first.

You can continue this approach until one opponent is defeated, then repeat with the second. Once you have mastered this concept you should have the same success rate against two as you do one. This tactic is simple in concept though difficult in execution. We will look further into this in future guides.

This approach can be extended to more than two opponents and becomes easier if the terrain is diverse, with features such as holes, ditches, hills, streams and trees. Also easier if you are fit, as movement is of prime importance in exploiting the advantages that can be obtained from obstacles.

Drill 19 continued

Red exchanges shield for sword on the outside while half stepping forward...

...and thrusts with the sword in Right Ox with a half steps forward, attacking Blue's right shoulder, Blue half steps back and parries with the Shield Parry 2.

Red makes a full step diagonally forward to the right, while covering the attacking lines with his shield...

...and makes Attack 4 to the left thigh. The usual pattern repeated as required.

SECTION IX. 4.

SECTION X – CONCLUSIONS
COMMON ERRORS

Here we present some of the more common mistakes that have been seen at seminars. It is hoped that by providing examples, you can eliminate them from your practice and combats.

Common Error 1
Bending the wrist in a thrust. This tends to make the thrust weak, and also the wrist. This means that you can be easily disarmed, and also injured.

Common Error 2
Locking the arm out in a thrust. Apart from being dangerous this could also injure the elbow after many repetitions.

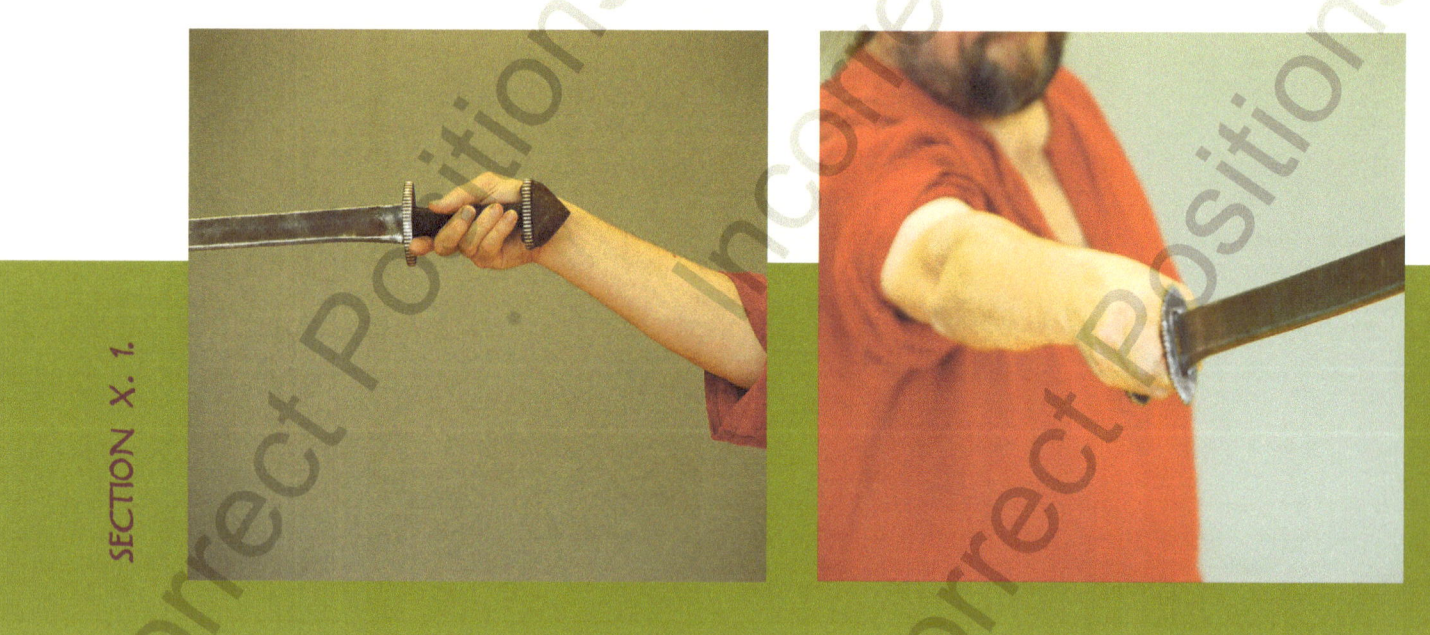

Common Error 3
Parrying a thrust upwards. This is a universal error and could bring about a serious injury if you are not wearing face and throat protection. It is most dangerous when done against a spear thrust.

Common Error 4
Not protecting the hand when fighting with a full body target. This failing is often not even noticed by the defender or attacker. If the hand is exposed, try to hit it!

Common Error 5
Fighting with the shield against the chest. This sort of defence is often seen in combats with rule systems that do not have the full body target. In real life someone would just stick a spear through the shield into the person's body.

Common Error 6
Lazy shield use. While attacking, some people forget to use the shield at all. This is seen very often in novice swordsmen. The counter is all too obvious.

Common Error 7
Parrying a weapon well down from the point. It seems logical that the earlier you parry a thrust the better the protection, but this is false in many cases. Reaching to parry earlier, by going further down the weapon usually means the point hits before your parry takes effect. This is very noticeable here using a spear.

AN EXCHANGE OF BLOWS – AN EXAMPLE OF A FIGHT

This is the final example of an exchange of blows in this series. Unfortunately presenting a fight in a few simple pictures taken from one side it is difficult to show what is actually going on in all its complexity. So the reader must realise that this representation of the fight is missing a great deal of the small movements, the technical repetition, the jockeying for position and a host of other mechanisms that take place during such an engagement. We always try to simplify what we show for ease of learning, for that we can make no apology.

Fights can last a few seconds or last many minutes depending upon a host of factors. The quick kill is usually made by executing a single combination that the defender cannot cope with at their level of development. This can literally be a 1 second bout! A fight between people that have developed a good standard of defence can take many combinations before something gives and someone has been hit. This is usually because one of the combatants has made a mistake. Even very good fighters can lose this way, and it is usually because they start thinking mid fight which means the automatic mode that

Red starts in Middle Guard, Blue starts in Guard Position 2.

Blue makes a step forward and attacks the open left shoulder of Red with Attack 2. Red steps a half step backward parrying with shield. Blue's right arm is exposed to counter attack.

they should fight with has been lost. Sometimes the fighter must try and work out a solution to a problem on the spot, though it should be as short a period as possible.

Red takes advantage of Blue's shield being out of place to step diagonally forward and cuts down against Blue's left leg. Blue withdraws the leg by stepping back.

Blue steps forward and makes a cut from above against Red's leg. Red reacts by stepping back and parrying with the shield, while bringing his sword into the Ox position on the right hand side.

In combats there are always subtle changes going on that even the fighters are not consciously aware of. Covering main lines of attack with the shield while executing an attack, preparing an exchange of weapon, switching balance, pushing in physically or yielding where appropriate, pulling out and re-entering on a new line with a new attack, are all actions that are borne of long hours training and heaps of experience. A fight is a contest of wills on every level, and victory usually goes to those who have tried everything in practice many times and have mastered themselves. The willingness to give up the initiative because the position is a dead end, rarely occurs to people who's ego is pushing them for a win at any cost. The warrior within must bend to the requirements of the fight: retreat, turn, give and accept; the warrior can do everything.

We can only hope that this series has awoken the warrior within you. Maybe one day we will cross swords on the battlefield.

SECTION X. 2.

Red steps forward in Right Ox and thrusts to Blue's left shoulder, Blue blocks with the shield face.

Red lifts the point of his sword over the rim of the shield, while stepping forward. This is a subtle change of line which is hard to see. Blue should move the shield over to his right and block the line. Unfortunately Red is too quick!

Red quickly switches the thrust to the right shoulder while stepping forward to the left with the weight on the left leg and lands the attack, winning the fight.

SECTION X. 2.

CONCLUSIONS

We have covered in these three books all that is needed to become a competent fighter with Viking era sword and shield. We could have expanded each book and easily doubled the work load though this would lead to a daunting amount of material to deal with. We feel it is best to leave the student to explore the other paths we have suggested in their own way, and at their own pace.

The way you use what you have learnt and the myriad ways you combine it will shape your own style of fighting. We cannot help you with that as everyone is an individual. We can only hope to provide you with sign posts to guide you on your way. The greatest of these sign posts is control, for once you can control your sword and yourself in any situation, surely you have nothing to fear in the fight. This can only be achieved by diligent practice with and without a partner, and by repeating the basics time and time again. If you wish to be excellent then train the basics because in a fight that is what you will rely on time and time again.

These books are planned over a long period with

Fighting with sword and axe

Fighting with two swords

care and forethought, even so we may have missed something that you thought important. Please send us your ideas and thoughts on our products so we can improve over time. Arts of Mars books is committed to producing good quality books on many different subjects. We have planned other titles for the future of Viking era combat. If you think of something of interest please drop us a line, the more interest a subject gets the more we will push it to the front of the queue.

The next series of three books will be the Viking Sword and Shield: Advanced Guides, which will be expanded by six more volumes covering all the common weapons of that period. See the pictures below to see what we could have lined up for you.

We wish you a pleasant and rewarding experience in the world of historical European Viking era combat.

Fighting with two handed weapons

Fighting with spear and shield

FURTHER MATERIAL

Help Videos
To give more help for those who find learning from a book difficult we have placed some videos on our Youtube channels which deal with Viking era sword and shields. We have set up a special channel for Viking era material.

Our channels are called:
- Viking Guide Books
- Arts Of Mars Historical European Martial Arts

Find out more information at the following web site or sign up for our newsletter:
www.artsofmars.com

Watch out for our **online learning program** starting in 2014.

Books and DVDs by
Arts of Mars Books
Publishing House
Germany

All Books are available at **Swordexperts.com**

**Viking Sword
and Shield Fighting
Beginners Guide Level 1**

Price: 24,90 Euro

This is a full colour step by step guide for beginners on how to fight safely with a Viking sword and shield. This book is useful for people interested in Historical European Martial Arts, Stage Combat, and Re-enactors. It describes techniques, drills and common errors, in a simple but clear way using the unique Timeline system, so that people can follow each step easily and quickly. The author Colin Richards has 34 year experience in fighting with weapons and especially the Viking sword and shield combination. He has taught well over 2500 people in this combat art. The book also includes rules of engagement and a sample fight, and where to obtain good reliable equipment for this activity.

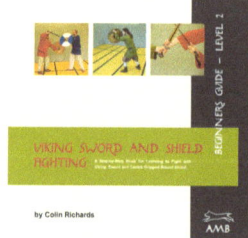

**Viking Sword
and Shield Fighting
Beginners Guide Level 2**

Price: 29,90 Euro

The study of Viking fighting is by and large a personal quest as there is little known about the fighting style of those times. This book attempts to bring together the information handed down to us by Medieval and Renaissance masters of arms, and combine it with the authors 33 years experience of combat with these weapons. This combined knowledge is distilled into a series of simply presented, though comprehensive lessons designed to develop the skills of novice and experienced warriors alike. Filled with tactical tips and practical advice this book series brings a new dimension to step by step guides.

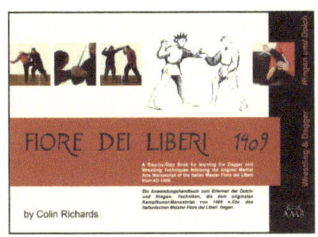

Fiore dei Liberi 1409
Wrestling & Dagger
Ringen & Dolch

Price: 44,95 Euro

This book covers the Wrestling and Dagger techniques of Fiore Dei Liberi from the 'Getty' version of the 'Fior di Battaglia'. Included is a selection of the 'Pisani-Dossi' 'Flos Duellatorum' dagger techniques. All techniques are described in both English and German languages. This is a step by step guide to the wrestling and dagger techniques of Fiore Dei Liberi using a new approach. Using a unique Timeline system, the photographs in the book detail the stages of each technique as they occur in time, with a separate close up focus on hand and foot movements, each positioned in the Timeline at the correct place. The whole book has been designed around the needs of the student who wishes to learn the actual techniques. This system allows the reader to follow the whole technique from start to finish and to learn it. This book is full colour and has approximately 900 pictures and 208 sides sewn, hard back, protected paper designed to survive the hard wear and tear of the training hall!

Fiore dei Liberi 1409
Medieval Sword fighting
Student Guide Level 1

Price: 39,90 Euro

The Italian Martial Arts Master Fiore dei Liberi wrote his highly effective fighting techniques down for future generations to delve into the mysteries of the world of knightly combat. We present this valuable cultural heritage for those interested in historical combat in three DVDs, the first of which "Student Guide - Level 1" includes the following: Gripping the Sword, Breathing Technique, Stance Turning, Tactical Stepping, Basic Guard Positions, Cutting with the Sword, Thrusting with the Sword, Distance, Single Person Drills and Partner Drills! This DVD is a must for those who seriously want to learn the fundamental principles of Fiore dei Liberi's Longsword Combat System. This DVD is structured for easy learning for both single persons and groups and is finely tuned to help any experience level from absolute beginner to advanced practitioner.

Joachim Meyers
Kunst des Fechtens

Price: 39,90 Euro

Joachim Meyer wrote an impressive text book on the state of German martial arts in the second half of the 16th Century. At the time in which it was printed, it was an important and pioneering work, for it was the first book of its kind, which was actually written for students of swordsmanship and described a systematic learning system. The author Alexander Kiermayer has transferred the work of Joachim Meyer in the modern German language and has processed it so that it is easily accessible for the modern reader. The original unique wood-cuts, are also included in the translation. To allow the reader an easier understanding of the text by Joachim Meyer, the corresponding relevant parts have been extracted from the woodcuts and arranged next to the descriptive text. Thus, the book includes within the 240 pages 189 illustrations from contemporary woodcuts, and graphics.

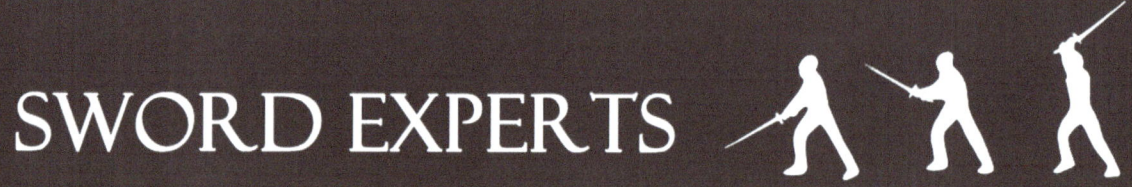

SWORD EXPERTS

**You
want to learn Historical European Martial Arts**

**We
have got the equipment!**

**Longswords • Single Handed Swords • Daggers
Fencing Masks • Gloves • Groin and Breast Protection
Throat Protection • Jackets
Books • DVD and more**

Supplied by
Arts of Mars Books
Allstar • Peter Regenyei • PBT • Purple Heart Armouries • Samurai Sports
Seelenschmiede • SPES • The Knightshop and more...

**Fast Delivery World Wide!
Best Price Guaranty!
High Quality Standard!
Top Offers!**

www.Swordexperts.com

www.ingramcontent.com/pod-product-compliance
Ingram Content Group UK Ltd.
Pitfield, Milton Keynes, MK11 3LW, UK
UKHW060138240426
12048UKWH00003B/84